# PETER THE ROCK

*For Nick and Nikos.*

*May you always live
in a world that is
intelligent and tolerant.*

# PETER THE ROCK

## WHAT THE ROMAN PAPACY WAS, AND WHAT IT MIGHT BECOME

## ROBERT CROTTY

SPECTRUM PUBLICATIONS MELBOURNE 2015

First published in Australia in 2015 by Spectrum Publications Pty Ltd
a: PO Box 75, Richmond, Victoria, Australia 3121
t: (+61) 1300 540 736, f: (+61) 1300 540 737
e: spectrum@spectrumpublications.com.au
www.spectrumpublications.com.au

Cover Design: xy arts
Typesetting by Spectrum Publications Pty Ltd
Typeface: Goudy, Friz Quadrant

ISBN: 978-0-86786-097-9 (13)


National Library of Australia Cataloguing-in-Publication entry

Creator:      Crotty, Robert B., author.

Title:        Peter the rock : what the Roman papacy was, and what it might
              become / Robert Crotty.

ISBN:         9780867860979 (paperback)

Notes:        Includes bibliographical references and index.

Subjects:     Catholic Church--History.
              Catholic Church--Doctrines.
              Papacy--History.
              Popes--Primacy--History.
              Popes--Infallibility.

Dewey Number: 262.13

Figures:

# CONTENTS

# INTRODUCTION

When he was an old man in his nineties, Pope Leo XIII reprimanded his Secretary of State, who dared to question one of his decisions, with the Latin words: *Ego sum Petrus* ('I am Peter'). The Secretary of State immediately caved in.

Who was 'Peter'?

This book grapples with the question of the Bishops of Rome, the Popes, who have claimed to this day that they are 'Peter', that they are the Rock of the Catholic Church, just as the apostle Simon was given the name 'Peter' (*Petros* in Latin, *Cephas* in Aramaic), meaing 'The Rock'. What does it mean for a church leader to be 'Peter'? More importantly, is there a need for this 'Peter' to continue in the twenty-first century?

The book will cover the beginning of the line of Popes, or the Papacy, and deal with some of the individuals who have ruled the Roman Catholic Church for two thousand years.

At this point terminology needs to be clarified. The Christian group with its centre in Rome was first called 'Catholic' (*katholikos* or 'universal' in Greek) in the early second century by the bishop of Antioch, Ignatius. He used it to distinguish this group from other Christian groups, not aligned with Rome. When the Eastern Christian Church split from Rome in 1054, the church in Rome retained the title 'Catholic', while the Eastern Church used the title 'Orthodox' or 'right-thinking'. Finally, after the Reformation in the sixteenth century, Rome continued the use of Roman Catholic Church to distinguish itself from the churches of the Reformers. In more recent times the terms 'Roman Catholic Church' and 'Catholic Church' have both been used in official Vatican documents. Where I use 'the Church' in this book, it is shorthand for the Roman Catholic Church. It does not mean that I hold that the Roman Catholic Church is the only Church or the universal Church, just as references to the Eastern Orthodox Church do not imply acceptance that they alone are right-thinking.

There have been many books written on the Papacy. Most have been historical; some have been theological treatises. Some have been in favour of the institution, with awe for its longevity. Some have been antithetical

to it, seeing it as an out-dated office, often populated by unworthy leaders.
This will be a different book.

## Some General Information

The Pope is regarded by Roman Catholics as the Supreme Head of the Roman Catholic Church. In fact, accepting that teaching is part of the definition of being a Roman Catholic.

The popular name used to describe the Bishop of Rome, Pope, means 'Father'. Although there are several claims to its earlier usage among the Bishops of Rome, it only became a commonly used term in the eleventh century. A number of Orthodox Church leaders up to the present day, particularly the Coptic Patriarch of Alexandria, have also claimed the same title. In the Western Church (and in the West generally), its normal usage applies exclusively to the Bishop of Rome

The Pope bears other titles that reveal his pre-eminence in the Catholic Church: His Holiness (derived from The Holy One, a Hebrew word for God), Vicar of Christ, Successor of Saint Peter, Prince of the Apostles, *Pontifex Maximus* (Latin for Supreme Pontiff, the title of the Roman Chief Priest in ancient Roman religion), Archbishop of the Roman Province, Primate of Italy, Patriarch of the West, Sovereign of the State of Vatican City, *Servus Servorum Dei* ('Servant of the servants of God'), *Pastor Pastorum* ('Pastor of the pastors'; the Pope usually signs himself with the addition of 'P.P.').

There has been considerable popular interest in the Papacy in recent years. To a great extent this has been fostered by mass media output. With easy access to multimedia, immediate transmission of events and some great moments of acclamation and scandal within the papal circle, the Papacy has been open to scrutiny in a way that was impossible even sixty years ago. In the reign of Pius XI (1922-1939), for example, most Catholic people outside Italy would not have known much more about the Pope than his name. His successor, however, Pius XII, was widely reported in the media and regarded as a very public and saintly figure. Although Italian, and Italy was part of the Axis enemy for many Catholics, he was said to have risen above any national interests during the Second World War. He was not only fluent in twelve languages, but knowledgeable in a myriad number of theological and natural sciences.

This media knowledge was manipulated; the public knew nothing of his sometimes unsuccessful international political dealings, his questionable involvement in halting the Holocaust, his illusions of grandeur, his constant hypochondria and, towards the end of his life, his claims to mystical experiences, visions and oracular knowledge on all the sciences. Since that time the Popes have become even more public and human figures, sometimes too public and too human.

The Papacy itself, particularly on the occasion of the death of one Pope and the election of another, continues to intrigue and interest not only Catholics but many others. The media have a field day. How is the Pope's body consigned to the earth (unless like Benedict XVI and two others, the Pope resigns), how is the Conclave (from Latin *con clave*, 'with a key', the official name for the consultative meeting where electors are shut in to elect a successor) convoked, how does the voting system work, what happens when a final decision is made? The world community was intrigued by the front-page media reports of the mostly outmoded pageantry which was such an essential part of the election of the last several Popes.

Hence it is legitimate to ask even further: how did such a grandiose office of Pope come to be? Should it continue?

### *The Church Story*

The official Church Story (the account that is still officially taught within the Roman Catholic Church) runs thus:

1. Jesus appointed his disciple Peter as Head of the Twelve Apostles during his lifetime.
2. After the death of Jesus, Peter was confirmed in this office of headship by the resurrected Jesus and the post was extended over the entire Christian Church.
3. Peter, after apostolic work in Jerusalem and Antioch, went to Rome and founded the Christian Church there and became its first bishop, until he was executed under the emperor Nero. He is buried in Rome, under Saint Peter's Basilica.
4. Any successor to Peter as Bishop of Rome is also, as a consequence, successor to his role of headship: the successors of Peter in an unbroken line, should be accorded the same role of Head of the universal Church as was Peter, and their universal authority acknowledged.

This is a neat Church Story, and we will examine it in detail later. Most Catholics would accept all the above four statements; many non-Catholic Christians would claim to differ on the fourth. However, it will be demonstrated in this book that the first three statements are not historically valid and the seemingly logical conclusion in the fourth point must therefore be questioned, as it stands.

## *Methodology used in the book*

The book's research is based on Critical Inquiry. Critical Inquiry is a search for knowledge with a completely open mind. The facts are allowed to filter through the mind. But the knowledge that is sought is such that it should give rise to action, to a search for human freedom. The institution of the Papacy is mysterious and it has been hailed as both a divine necessity by some and a burden by others. It is a good topic for Critical Inquiry. The question is: how to decide which way to make use of the knowledge gained in the Inquiry? The Conclusion will try to do that.

The project will use the method of historical research (although it does not intend simply to catalogue historically some or all of the Popes), but it will also use the method of phenomenology of religion. Phenomenology of religion stands back from the many manifestations of religion in the world, present and past, and tries to see some order and coherence in them.

Phenomenology of religion looks at the various aspects of human religion (such as a ritual dance, a belief in a High God, a religious taboo against eating pork) from the point of view of the believer (although the phenomenologist, at least while working as such, 'brackets out' any personal belief commitment). The phenomenologist breaks down what is experienced in the research into component parts and studies them across various religious traditions. The aim is to understand not just the facts about religions but its living heart, something that obviously stimulates and nurtures a group of believers.

The Papacy is a religious phenomenon and an interesting, even intriguing, one and can be studied in this way. It does not stand isolated in Roman Catholic belief. There are similar headship institutions in other religions. In order to apply phenomenology of religion, we must first agree on a statement regarding religion. For this purpose, we begin with the concept of human culture.

We are surrounded by secular culture in everyday life. Culture consists of the organised ways of thinking, acting and valuing proper to a group of humans. Secular culture allows human beings to find order amid common human experience, to explain historical events, to solve problems regarding their own identity. We are able to walk down the street of a city, to pass certain people by and to greet others in conversation, to share a meal and communicate, to achieve a day's work because we share a common culture with these many people. We feel comfortable in our own cultural setting (whereas we may not feel comfortable in a North African one).

However, there are times when people find themselves faced with profound ignorance that does not provide easy answers, with the experience of suffering (my friends, relatives and even I myself may experience physical and mental problems) and with the problem of evil (why are children abused? why do innocent people suffer and die? why are there tsunamis?). These things can threaten an ordered, cultural world.

At this point, where secular culture cannot cope, there is an urgent need for something more – a religious culture. A 'religious culture' could include the living world religions, indigenous religions such as the many Aboriginal Australian religions, religious sects, Marxism, Humanism and so on. The religious person, by means of this religious culture, can make sense of the world, of others and self in terms of Ultimacy.

Ultimacy is ultimate order, where everything fits in perfectly, as against everyday order, where most everyday things fit into some order. A religious culture provides us with a focus by which we can see everything in relationship with Ultimacy. Whereas we can manage with our secular culture to get by day-to-day, there are times when we need to see the Big Picture. All humans have the inborn capacity to do this. All human persons who are capable of independent thought and are not mentally handicapped to any significant degree should therefore be designated as 'religious persons', although the 'religion' of some of these people might not necessarily be recognised as a religion in the conventional sense. Some might follow a nature religion with a mixture of Buddhist meditation and Christian belief in an afterlife.

Humans feel that there is a great gulf between themselves and Ultimacy or ultimate order, which is the understanding of the world, of other people, the meaning of life and death, the reason for suffering. Religion is about bridging that gulf.

With everyday culture (say Chinese culture or European culture) there is always the possibility of ethnocentrism, the idea that my culture, with its particular ways of thinking and acting, is the only true culture. In fact, it is normal to think that the way I think and do things is the right way. There can be many intermediate steps until we put aside this ethnocentrism and come to multiculturalism, where we recognise that all human cultures are true, despite being different. It is something the same with religion.

There are three main highpoints in the scale, with possibilities in between, when we examine the attitudes of humans towards religious culture.

- *Exclusivism* is the attitude that only one particular religious culture is valid, all others are mistaken.
- *Inclusivism* describes the view that one religious culture is certainly valid, but that other religious cultures, but not all, may share – completely, partially, even perhaps inadequately – the truth of the one valid religious culture.
- *Pluralism* would maintain that all religious cultures are acceptable. They all can achieve the same purpose of putting a group into contact with Ultimacy, with ultimate meaning. Why choose one rather than another? This would be due to the family into which the person was born, subsequent education, the chance events of a person's life story.

We need now to analyse this religious culture, a religion, in broader detail. As was said above, religion is about bridging the gulf between a human group and Ultimacy. The central phenomenon of any religion is not its sacred text (if it should be a literate society), nor its ethical system, nor its doctrinal teaching, but its religious experience, the quality of human reaction that is aroused by a deep-felt moment of contact with Ultimacy.

We can take the example of Islam. Its sacred story recounts that at a certain moment Muhammad, while deep in meditation on a hill outside Mecca, was enabled to contact what he interpreted as Ultimacy. He identified Ultimacy by means of *al 'ilah*, 'The God' or Allah. For him *al 'ilah* became a new religious focus that gave him access to Ultimacy. By means of *al 'ilah* he was able to comprehend Ultimacy. He described this experience as *islam*, absolute submission and an awareness of human frailty in the presence of Ultimacy. He thereby achieved an ultimate order in his life. Muhammad's religion is the religion of *islam* or 'submission' and its adherents are *muslims* or 'people submitted' to Allah.

But Muhammad might have died without revealing how he had achieved his personal contact with Ultimacy; he might have kept it as a personal secret. In that case, there would have been no followers. However, he left a body of myths (or sacred stories, not to be confused with the popular use of the term meaning untruths) and accounts of rituals (or religious ceremonies) which could allow his followers bring ultimate meaning and direction into their own lives. Islamic myth and ritual are the principal means by which a Muslim can contact al'ilah.

A similar process can be identified with all religions. Religious experience is brought about by sacred myth and ritual. Myth or sacred story is the way religious people speak and communicate with each other. All religious traditions have a fund of such stories. Importantly though, sacred stories are not necessarily historical stories.

This type of mythical story is a metaphor that conveys the most profound spiritual truth, a truth not communicable by everyday language. It provides the essential features of a religious culture in story-form. But myth does more than recount facts about life. It recreates the original 'world' of the 'time of the beginnings', in which the way of life of a human group, the fund of its common understandings and its principal values, were established.

Myths convey information to the group about how the world came to be ('creation' or beginning stories), about how humans were separated from Ultimacy (stories about a First Fall or a cosmic tragedy), about the possibility that the group can regain contact with Ultimacy (for example, the sacred stories of Founders of religions and stories of atonement), about the possibility of final reconciliation with Ultimacy (eschatological myths).

Myth or sacred story is organically connected with religious ritual. Ritual is a ceremony, a sacred drama. Rather than recounting the deepest truths, the persons involved in ritual act out these truths. A core ritual is the re-enactment of that past event, when contact was initially made between a Founder or founding group and Ultimacy. But ritual, like myth, can only be understood when it is acknowledged to be essentially and inextricably connected with religious experience.

For example, the Jewish Passover is the dramatic, ritual-portrayal of the Exodus out of Egypt, as recounted in the sacred book of Judaism, the Torah. This was achieved, Jews believe, by the God of Israel, known by the personal name of Yahweh[1]. Performing the ritual of Passover brings the past Exodus-event into the present for the believing group. It is as if a particular group of Jews, gathered in the home on the festival of Passover, eating unleavened bread and drinking wine, becomes part of the group of

Moses and the Passover people and personally experiences the saving, guiding, comforting presence of the God of Israel, Yahweh. That Exodus-experience was considered to be the founding experience of Judaism, and celebrating Passover brings the experience of the past event into the present. Yahweh becomes their focus on Ultimacy.

Likewise for Christians, the celebration of the sacrament of Baptism is the dramatic, ritual re-enactment of being incorporated in the community that is ruled by Jesus. Jesus as the envoy of The Father[2] came to establish a believing group. The Christian must undergo the initiation of passing through the waters of the Sea of Reeds, as the Israelites did at the beginning of the Exodus, and also the passing through of the waters of Jordan, as the Israelites did to enter the Land of Promise. But more, Jesus was baptised to become part of John the Baptist's group and this was what led to the Jesus-group. According to this way of thinking, the baptised become members of the people of the full promise: the Christians.

Once more, myth together with ritual, provide the context for a religion's particular experience; it is the moment of contact; this experience reveals that the group has made contact with Ultimacy. This provides ultimate meaning and gives ultimate direction to the participants. That is why humans have religions.

Let us return to the Muhammad example. Muhammad was introduced to a profound religious experience that allowed him to see everything in ultimate perspective. He found *al 'ilah* and through that focus he contacted Ultimacy. Imbued with the religious experience of submissiveness, *islam*, he was satisfied, but the question was left open, as was pointed out earlier, as to whether his experience could be repeated by others. If not, then Muhammad's new, individual religious culture, personally satisfying as it undoubtedly was, would be spontaneously aborted. There would have been a Muhammad, but not an Islam.

This is the vital point about the establishment of a religion. Can the founding religious experience be replicated by others? Can the Founder, who has already experienced Ultimacy, have a succession and successors? 'Founders' are like great artists. Most people have deep experiences of nature and human relationships in their lifetime. These experiences are usually occasional, personal and indescribable. The artist is that rare gifted individual who is able to use a medium – words, paint, musical sound – to communicate a deep, personal experience to others.

Similarly, the religious 'Founder' is the person (or sometimes a group) who has undergone a personal contact with Ultimacy, but is then able to construct a system which can convey the ability to achieve this original religious experience to others. That system would consist basically of a collection of myths and rituals, sometimes linked to a sacred text in literate societies. The system can be called an intermediary system, because it brings about mediation between the human group and Ultimacy. This is analogous to a group of sensitive people who, through an artist's great work of art, come into contact with Meaning in the world. The group cannot achieve this on their own, they can do so by means of the structure that has been set up.

This intermediary system organises other religious phenomena. Its driving mechanism, the recital of myths and performance of rituals, produces a profound religious experience, considered to be a replica of the founder's own original experience. The same mechanism also establishes a social structure, a group of like-minded people who share more or less the same experience and, like all societies, its members will be graded into different religious roles. The group learns what is expected as far as ethical behaviour and thinking is concerned; it is controlled by a binding list of essential beliefs and, in literate societies, by a sacred text.

We can now outline the main facets of this intermediary system. Mediation, linking a human group to Ultimacy, allows a group of humans to see life from an ultimate perspective. Depending upon the group's culture and world view, the gulf between the ultimate order of things and the human group will be perceived as more or less wide. From the side of Ultimacy the gulf can be partially bridged by Other-worldly Intermediaries such as divine children and divine messengers; from the side of the human group it will be bridged by This-worldly Intermediaries such as sacred persons, kings, prophets or heroes. The two sides of the system are intended to ensure that the human group makes contact with the sacred focus. This focus then allows the group to come into contact with Ultimacy.[3]

All of this can be entered into a schematic model:

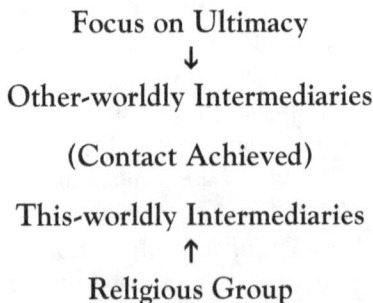

**Focus on Ultimacy**

↓

**Other-worldly Intermediaries**

**(Contact Achieved)**

**This-worldly Intermediaries**

↑

**Religious Group**

The focus on Ultimacy is usually, but not always, depicted as a High God, creator of the cosmos and determiner of human destiny. However the focus can also be a group of gods or a more indistinct god-like structure.

In short, religion is the means by which humans make contact with Ultimacy. The way they depict their focus on Ultimacy (a God like Allah for Islam, a pantheon of gods for the ancient Greeks, a great world-soul for some Hindus, Dreamtime Beings for Aboriginal Australians, the ideal of Humanity-within-a-good-world-order for Humanists) differs. We can now more clearly ask: is one depiction of a focus on Ultimacy the only right one for everyone (exclusivism), or is one focus certainly right and some others close enough (inclusivism) or are all foci on Ultimacy, which presumably work, right and it is just a matter of personal preference (pluralism)? This book will not be deciding on that question, interesting as it is. Hopefully, there should be thinking room in the book for exclusivists, inclusivists and pluralists to feel at home.

When a religious group does make contact with Ultimacy, via its focus, then there is a religious experience (as was said, of submission or *islam* for Islam, of loving-kindness and 'chosenness' for the Jews, of *agape* or love of God-and-others for Christians, of universal knowledge for some indigenous religions). That religious experience is generated by Sacred Story and Religious Ritual leading to the identification of the Other-worldly Intermediary (or Intermediaries) and then allowing the human community to use this contact as a focus and thus being able to contact Ultimacy.

The important point that must be made is that, if a religion is to be successful and put the human group into contact with Ultimacy by means of the focus, then that experience will be believed to be the replication of what the Founder or Founders experienced. For the system to work there has to be replication and succession. Succession is the vital aspect for the establishment of a religion.

Returning one more time to Islam, we know that the focus on Ultimacy was *al 'ilah* or Allah. Allah, it is firmly believed in Islam, produced the sacred book of the Qur'an. Its words were his words (which goes a step further than the notion of Inspiration of the Scriptures in Judaism and Christianity). So the structure of Islam emerges:

Focus on Ultimacy: Allah

↓

Other-worldly Intermediary: the Divine Qur'an

(Contact Achieved)

This-worldly Intermediary: Muhammad and the successors of Muhammad who interpret the written Qur'an

↑

Community of Islam

Dissension within Islam is not over Muhammad, but over the identification of the successors of Muhammad.[4]

Christianity, whether it is regarded as the one true religion or as a true religion among many others, follows the same cultural pattern as described above. There is a focus (Father or 'abba), Other-worldly Intermediaries (The Word of God, the Spirit of God, the Divine Jesus) and This-worldly Intermediaries. As with Islam, it is the specific identification of the This-worldly Intermediaries that has split Christianity asunder.

So, this book intends to explain how the phenomenon of the Pope came into being and how it came to be such an essential part of the Church Story. Is the Pope of the time the This-worldly Intermediary for all Christians? What is undeniable is that the Papacy, however it came to be, has exerted enormous influence on historical events, on human practice, on cultural and religious development throughout two thousand years of human history. It is an institution that deserves documentation and explanation. But the question that is being asked today is: should the Papacy and its claim to be the This-worldly Intermediary continue?

*This book does not have an agenda beyond presenting the meaning and the related story of the Papacy. In particular, it intends to research what 'Peter' means and has meant in the past as the basis of the institution of the Papacy. Although the Conclusion will make some suggestions about the future, readers can read the book and make up their own minds on any future action that might need to be taken.*

*The research will not challenge the fact that the Christian*

Church was certainly founded on the memory and tradition of Jesus. However, there were intermediate stages before a Christian Church emerged: a proliferation of Jesus-movement groups after his death, linked in some way to Judaism; the failure of some to flourish; the ability of one Jesus-movement group in Rome to break with Judaism and attain dominance. All of this has repercussions for a discussion on the Papacy.

Clearly Jesus as Founder of Christianity needs to be explained. Jesus can only be understood against the backdrop of Judaism; he was Jewish and must have thought like at least some Jews of the time. For this purpose the Hebrew Scriptures need to be examined carefully, if the backdrop to Jesus' thought and work is to be understood.

Then, the big question: what was the Succession from Jesus to Christian Church? what was the succession from Peter to later heads?

So, logically, we begin with Judaism, the Jewish Story, and move from there to the Jesus Story.

## NOTES

The book will not provide a history of all the Popes in sequence. For such historical outlines the following can be recommended.

Kelly, J. (1968), *The Oxford Dictionary of the Popes*, A. and C. Black: London

Bunson, M. (1995), *The Pope Encyclopedia. An A to Z of the Holy See*, Crown Trade Paperbacks: New York

Duffy, E. (1997), *Saints and Sinners. A History of the Popes*, Yale University Press: New Haven

Collins, P. (2000), *Upon this Rock. The Popes and their Changing Role*, MUP: Melbourne

Paul Collins has also written an earlier book dealing with the very question of the need for change in the papacy.

Collins, P. (1997), *Papal Power. A Proposal for Change in Catholicism's Third Millennium*, HarperCollins Religious: Melbourne.

For the ideas on Culture used in the Introduction (and they will be used again in the Conclusion) see:

Barbour, Ian (1974), *Myths, Models and Paradigms*, Harper and Row: New York.

Geertz, Clifford (1973), *The Interpretation of Cultures*, Basic Books: New York,
which contains his essay defining religion as:

(1) a system of symbols which acts to (2) establish powerful, pervasive, and long-lasting moods and motivations in men by (3) formulating conceptions of a general order of existence and (4) clothing these conceptions with such an aura of factuality that (5) the moods and motivations seem uniquely realistic.

A more formal treatment of my thinking on the structures within religion can be found in:

Crotty, R. (1995), 'Towards Classifying Religious Phenomena', *Australian Religion Studies Review*, 8, pp. 34-41.

# 1/
# THE JEWISH STORY –
# LITERARY ISRAEL

*I would like first to make clearer some of my own terminology about Stories and History.*

*There is a Jewish Story which is contained in the Hebrew Scriptures, also known by some Christians as the Old Testament (not always considered politically correct, as it is based on exclusivism). Details on the content of this Jewish Story will be forthcoming. Further in this chapter, I will use a more technical term for this Story – Literary Israel.*

*There is also a Jesus Story. In fact, there are a number of them. The official ones are contained in the four gospels of Matthew, Mark, Luke and John of the canonical (officially recognised) Christian Scriptures, also known as the New Testament. But we know of other Jesus Stories, particularly in the Gnostic Gospels. A Jesus Story relates events in which he was involved in a particular sequence or sayings in a literary convention. Later, I will normally use the technical term Literary Jesus for the numerous Jesus Stories. And I will summarise the many Jesus Stories by the singular term Jesus Story.*

*Finally, there is a Church Story. For the purposes of this book, the Church Story continues the Jesus Story to provide an account of the establishment and stabilisation of the early Church, with its centre in Rome. At no point does the Church Story openly contradict any of the official Jesus Stories, at least those which are contained in the four gospels. The Church Story that has come down to us begins in the Acts of the Apostles. It was extended and edited by other Christian writers, but we have only fragments of their works. Eusebius of Caesarea, an official in the employ of Constantine the Great, wrote an extensive Church Story based on the Acts and some of these early texts.*

*What must be made absolutely clear from this point is that neither Jewish Story nor Jesus Story nor Church Story is necessarily historically accurate*

The Church Story, including its description of the establishment and role of the Papacy, did not emerge out of nothing. It was based on the Jesus Story. But the Jesus Story was written within the living tradition of Judaism. Jesus was a Jew; his early disciples were Jews. Early writers interpreted subsequent events to formulate the Church Story. We need to start with what existed before the beginning of Christianity – the Jewish Story.

Most books on the history of Judaism, even up to the present-day usually include, as more or less historical fact, the Biblical stories of Abraham and his sons and their wives (The Ancestors), of Moses and the Exodus out of Egypt, of the Taking of the Land by the twelve tribes of Israel, of David and his son Solomon, and then the separate lines of kings (and one queen) in the north and south of the Palestinian area, the destruction of Jerusalem by the Babylonians and the Exile in Babylon, the restoration of the Jewish people and the rebuilding of their Temple and their struggles with Greeks and Romans down to Christian times. The primary source for this narration of events has always been the Hebrew Scriptures.[5]

Figure 1
The presumed 'history' of the people of Israel: Goshen (where the Twelve Tribes lived in Egypt); the path of the Exodus; Jerusalem which was taken from the Canaanites.

Until the nineteenth century these events, as related in the Hebrew Scriptures, were generally seen as deriving from a Golden Age. They were regarded as reports from a time when life was radically different to what modern people know, a time when wondrous natural events, miracles, bodily cures and exorcisms were commonplace, when angels and demons roamed the world. Any debate mainly concerned the manner in which Jews and Christians mined these Hebrew Scriptures for texts providing the foundations for their own practice and teaching.

Recent times have seen new literary approaches to the interpretation of the Hebrew Scriptures. There was first the recognition that they were based on pre-existing sources. The stories of creation and the early generations of humans in the book of Genesis were found to have parallels in the myths of other ancient literatures. The stories of the Ancestors, the Exodus, the Taking of the Land were found to contain duplications and discrepancies that pointed to the combination of several earlier documents or traditions. This was devastating news to many practising Jews and Christians and challenged the theory of Inspiration of the Scriptures by divine dictation to outstanding people like Moses, David and Solomon. Much re-thinking was required.

There followed an acknowledgement that the Hebrew Scriptures made use of literary forms other than history. There were, for example, stories that were similar to myth, legend, fable, poetry, wisdom-writing; occasionally but not always there was a type of history as found in other ancient Near Eastern literatures. Of vital importance, it was claimed that the texts needed to be read in these particular literary forms, perhaps not familiar to readers in modern times, and the process of writing and re-writing of the texts had to be charted in order for the meaning to be extracted.

Subsequently, there have been desperate attempts to prove that at least the historical outline of events in the Hebrew Scriptures was trustworthy, even if some practical details might be questioned. Archaeology and history were engaged to give fuller descriptions and dates to the Ancestors, the Exodus, the building of the two Temples, the reigns of the kings of Judah and Israel, the destruction of Jerusalem and the Exile of some of its citizens into Mesopotamia. Historical sources and archaeology could not always provide this information. However it was still maintained that while there might be debate over minor issues, the main events themselves (such as the Exodus from Egypt, the building of Solomon's Temple, the Exile of the citizens of Jerusalem) were sacrosanct, more or less as outlined in the Hebrew Scriptures.

But in time even the pivotal events fell under scrutiny. The archaeology of Jericho, whose walls were said to tumble when Joshua's soldiers blew the sacred trumpets, did not seem to indicate any destruction at the time proposed for the end of the Exodus; there was little or no evidence for any grandiose kingdom of David and Solomon or a magnificent Temple. By the middle of the twentieth century there was a move away from the emphasis on the past events of Judaism themselves as being bearers of meaning and teaching, to a stress on the Biblical text. The question was asked: what do the Hebrew Scriptures, with their literary forms and rhetorical structure, tell us? Whatever might historically have taken place in the past became less and less important.

As a result, there was to be a new development, in the latter part of the past century. It depended on the text-based approach just described above. It was a minimalist theory that recognised only a small amount of history in the biblical texts and placed the writing of scrolls, which were to be eventually incorporated into the Hebrew Scriptures, quite late in the history of the Near East.

Previously, it had been strongly maintained that systematic writing of the earliest forms of the Bible texts, the forerunners of the Torah, could be dated back to the time of David and Solomon. Texts were said to have been almost contemporary with the earliest events and certainly contemporary with later ones. These primary texts, it was said, were then edited time and again before being considerably expanded. Likewise, it had been maintained that the earliest texts of the Prophets dated to their own lifetimes, in both the northern and southern kingdoms, even if they too were later edited and expanded. The Psalms were mostly dated at that time to the song practices in the first Temple of Jerusalem.

The new approach has questioned most of this dating and certainly questioned more than ever the historicity of the Hebrew Scriptures. As a result, this minimalist theory also requires the religion of Judaism to be dated much later than had previously been accepted. According to the minimalists, Judaism did not begin with Abraham, not even with David, not with the writing prophets. On the contrary, they dated Judaism in and around the third century CE, during the time of the Hasmonean kings who succeeded the Maccabee warriors.[6]

I will make use of the terminology that I have developed elsewhere to describe what I see as the three facets of this approach: Literary Israel (The Jewish Story), Historical Israel, Biblical Israel.

### *Literary Israel*

There is first and most importantly a Literary Israel, the Jewish Story, contained in the amalgam of stories within the Hebrew Scriptures. Literary Israel is a sacred story that has its own chronology and its own succession of events, as chronicled in the earlier description above. The story includes its own sacred and non-sacred characters, who successively appear from Adam to Ezra, and it concludes its tale in the Greek period prior to Christian beginnings.

Literary Israel looks like this:
- Creation of World and Humanity by Yahweh, and Sin-stories (Adam and Eve, Cain and Abel, the Flood Generation, the Tower of Babel)
- The Ancestors: Abraham and Sarah, Isaac and Rebekah, Jacob/Israel and his four wives from whom are born twelve males who establish the Twelve Tribes of Israel

- Moses and the Exodus of the Twelve Tribes out of Egypt. They meet the God of Israel, Yahweh, on Sinai. The Taking of the Land of Canaan
- Judges rule the Land
- David becomes King and captures Jerusalem as the capital of a great Kingdom. He is succeeded by his son, Solomon, who builds the First Temple to Yahweh.
- The united Kingdom divides into two kingdoms, Israel in the north and Judah in the south, each with a line of separate kings.
- Northern Israel is destroyed
- Judah in the south is destroyed together with its First Temple in Jerusalem
- The people of Israel are exiled to Babylonia
- The Persians allow them to return to rebuild the Second Temple of Yahweh
- The Greeks overcome the Persians and challenge the religion of Yahweh
- The Hasmoneans, successors to the Maccabee family, who rebelled against the Greeks, reassert possession of Jerusalem and Judah. They cleanse the Second Temple.

This is the Jewish Story. We distinguish this Story from Historical Israel.

### *Historical Israel*

There is also an Historical Israel. It is the orderly description and explanation of the sequence of people and events in the areas later known as Judah, Israel and Samaria (and their neighbours), such as can be reliably reconstructed from various historical documents (not including the Bible, but including inscriptions and some other documentation from the time) and archaeology.

Hence, we know from inscriptions that there were at least eight northern kings (such as Omri, Jehu, and Menahem) and that they ruled from a city called Samaria. We know virtually nothing about their ethnic origins or their impact on world events. We know that the city of Samaria was destroyed by the Assyrians in the eighth century BCE, that the city of Jerusalem was destroyed by the Babylonians in the sixth century BCE.

This historical account, Historical Israel, would define an ancient entity called 'Israel' (since there are inscriptions naming it) and other kingdoms, of which we possess only a vague knowledge. From the early Iron Age, around 1200, this 'Israel' may have been the name of a geographical area or it may have been applied to a particular group of people. Certainly, in the highlands to the north, a kingdom called Israel eventually developed and was destroyed by the Assyrians in 722 BCE. That date is historically verified by documents, not the Bible. Perhaps the biblical writers had more sources on hand than we do (they did not have archaeological information), however they would have overlaid any sources with their own particular religious thought.

Outside of this northern 'Israel', what could possibly be concluded historically about Judah in the southern area around Jerusalem, for example? There were certainly a few overlaps between written record and biblical story: The Assyrian king Sennacherib's siege of Jerusalem when a Hezekiah was king is well attested in both Assyrian documents and the Bible; the Lachish ostraca, broken pottery on which inscriptions were written, tell of the Babylonian invasion into Judah in the sixth century BCE (that invasion is also in the Bible); there is an historical reference to the exiled Judean king, Jehoiachin (mentioned in the Bible), being given rations in the Babylonian court. There is also mention of other kings (such as Hezekiah) and Judean officials.

These are all references to an Historical Judah, but in its later times. What about the Ancestors, Moses, the Exodus out of Egypt, the Judges? We have no historical evidence. What about the earlier foundation of Jerusalem as the great Judean capital by King David and his son Solomon? There is one passing and uncertain reference to the 'House of David' in the south, but nothing as regards a kingdom in any inscription. The united kingdom of David and Solomon, covering an area of vast geographical proportions, as reported in the biblical text, exists only in Literary Israel not in Historical Israel. There is no historical evidence that the northern kingdom ever broke away from the south, as the biblical text narrates. The extra-biblical evidence points to the fact that southern Judah did not even exist at the period that 'Israel' did in the north. Archaeology in fact demonstrates that there was nothing like an independent administrative state or empire in the southern area until the eighth century BCE.

Jerusalem certainly became the capital of this southern kingdom, although the archaeology of Jerusalem is uncertain as to earlier populations and history. Possibly, Judah and Jerusalem increased in size as a result of the Assyrian destruction in the north. By the seventh century Judah may have included a sizeable northern Israelite population who had fled from the destruction. Matters would remain so until the attacks by the Babylonians destroyed Jerusalem in 586 BCE.

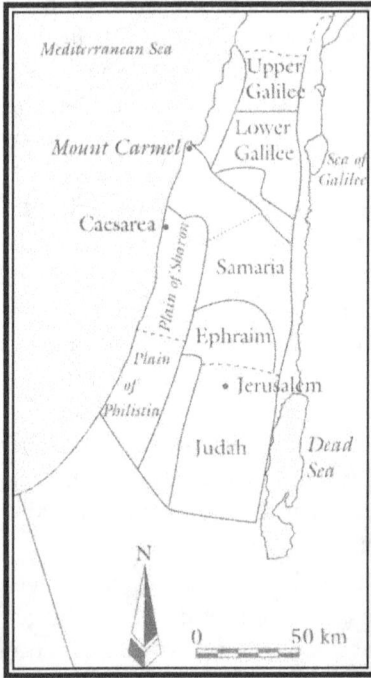

*Figure 2*
*Map of the historical area attributed to the northern Israelites, Judah and Galilee. The central location of Jerusalem is obvious.*

But this is all historical reconstruction, based on some evidence and educated interpretation. Historical Israel is very scrappy and incomplete.

### *Biblical Israel*

Finally, there is a Biblical Israel, the construct brought about by inserting Historical Israel (plus some questionable data that pretends to belong to Historical Israel) into Literary Israel to produce a hybrid.

Biblical Israel would explain the Burning Bush that was never consumed, as seen by Moses in the desert according to the book of Exodus, as ignited natural gas escaping from the soil. The phenomena of thunder and lightning that accompanied Yahweh's appearance on Mount Sinai described in Exodus and Deuteronomy were due to the rumblings and emissions of the volcanic area. Biblical Israel accounts would carefully chart the route of the Israelites during the Exodus, in order to put order into the events in the text. It would describe the Taking of the Land in the book of Joshua with the precision of an historian documenting the Normandy landings. Biblical Israel would give precise dates for all the kings of Israel and Judah mentioned in the books of Kings.

Going further, the Ten Plagues mentioned in the book of Exodus have provided a playground for the Biblical Israel cohort. The Nile being turned to blood is explained as red algae which poisoned fish life. The final plague, the Death of the Firstborn, has been attributed to Egyptian children eating polluted grain, rendered damp by the earlier Hail Plague and then contaminated by locust faeces from the Locust Plague and the grain being stored during the several days of Darkness from the ninth Plague, which was a sandstorm.

Even well-trained archaeologists, whose aim should be the presentation of Historical Israel, get involved instead in Biblical Israel.[7] Remnants of a building uncovered recently in Jerusalem were promptly dated to the tenth century and immediately attributed to David despite the absence of any inscription or other evidence. Presuming it is the palace of David, the Biblical Israel people go further: from the open top of this palace, David would have been able to see, across the ravine, the nude Bathsheba bathing in the evening on her house-top, as a lurid story in 1 Kings relates; the building would have been later extended by Solomon, because the account of that extension is in the biblical text.

So it goes on; inferences from archaeology and inscriptions are inserted into the biblical text by Biblical Israel scholars. This scholarly activity expands the usually dull archaeological reports; at the same time it considers itself to be substantiating the historicity of the Story in the Hebrew Scriptures. In fact, there are many competing versions of this Biblical Israel and some of the great scholars of the twentieth century have produced their own. It is a flawed endeavour and there is no advantage in producing a Biblical Israel.

For historians the study of the Historical Israel, using only historical sources, should be their aim. For students of religion and religious development, the principal aim has to be the study of Literary Israel, although they may need to consult Historical Israel.

To find out how Literary Israel, as contained in the Hebrew Bible, came into existence it is valid to interrogate history. That is an interesting question; it is not a matter of inserting history into the Story, but explaining the provenance of the Story. What we want to know is – at what stage could such a large body of written material have come into being?

## The Construction of Literary Israel

The numbers of Jerusalem citizens (and others living around the city) involved in the Exile in Babylonia after the destruction of the city by the Babylonians in 586 BCE could not have been as extensive and drastic as depicted in Literary Israel. The removal of almost an entire population to the East would have been logistically an impossible task. In reality, the majority of people must have been left where they were. Archaeology indicates that this was the case.

However, the ancient Near East changed. In 539 BCE the Babylonian Empire was taken over by the Persians who had moved inexorably towards the West, taking all in their path. During the fifth century BCE, there had been transfers of population in the opposite direction to that taken by the exiles – from Mesopotamia to Judah, now known as the Persian satrapy of Yehud. This administrative area of Yehud had been constructed as a province, comprising Jerusalem and the area adjacent to it, militarily under the control of the Persians. The Persians, according to accepted colonial practice, next transplanted a new population with a mandate to build a Temple and rebuild the city. These immigrants might or might not have had genealogical descent from the earlier exiled groups taken from the same area by the Babylonians.

However, Yehud shows an increase (by 25%) of new occupied settlements, in the form of unwalled villages, around this time. This archaeological data points to new settlers, not of the same stock as the earlier exiles who had moved west; former residents on their return would have been expected to go back to where they came from.

Most of these new villages had not been inhabited during the time of the monarchy and a quarter of them had never been occupied at all previously. A new population was being resettled. The colonists would have been transported specifically to promote the economic and political purposes of the Persians in Yehud. They would then have been settled into collectives, which became convenient units for Persian taxation. All of this was standard practice at the time.

At this point, historical interpretation, certainly based on historical sources and archaeology, should be allowed its head. These new social groupings in Yehud in about 400 BCE could well have given rise to the idea of the 'Twelve Tribes of Israel', formed not therefore in the Iron Age sometime after 1200 BCE, but in the Persian period in the sixth and fifth centuries BCE. The new immigrant population had not descended from 'Jacob' (also known as 'Israel') but from the new Persian arrangements for settling and controlling Yehud.

However that question might be decided, the newly-settled immigrants would have been required to make the land their own; their purpose was to carry out Persian directives and to ensure that the native population, who had never left the land, concurred. This undoubtedly set up conflict between the immigrants and the native population of Judah. The immigrants would have had instructions to establish themselves as a social enclave, setting up temple authorities, local managers and entrepreneurs. Importantly, the immigrant group would have included some literate people.

Within the city of Jerusalem, repaired and restored for their use, the newcomers must have established the cult of a new High God, Yahweh. There is an important distinction to be made here. Previously, there would have been several cults in both the north and south dedicated to a fertility and war god of the same name, Yahweh: city cults, dynastic cults, popular cults. This earlier religion of Yahweh, which can be reconstructed from archaeological remains, appears as a normal development from Canaanite religion. Yahweh was another form of the Canaanite god, 'El, and had a consort, Asherah. Historical Israel can verify that there would have been a number of other cults not dedicated to Yahweh (for example the worship of 'El himself, Ba'al, Hadad) and a number of other religious practices.

But this Yahweh of the earlier towns and villages was not the High God that came from the East, who was the creator of heaven and earth. What was the origin of this High God?

In this regard the question of the rebuilding of the Temple of Yahweh in Jerusalem, so prominent in the story of Literary Israel, becomes important. There was a particular form of 'temple' promoted by the Persians, difficult to understand if religion is seen as a separate institution within society, a common supposition today where Church and State are sedulously divided.

A temple was in ancient times not solely a religious institution. It was an institution that linked landowners and official temple personnel with the ruling élite. The ancient Near Eastern temple had been a common religious form, combining architecture, personnel and practice. Thus, it became the proprietor of public lands that were attributed to the deity as owner and it performed the function of a Treasury for the god's city. The king held his position and power by appointment from the temple deity. Hence, control of the Temple meant control of the economy and regulation of the social structure as well as supervision of religious ritual. Royalty and temple administration combined as the joint controllers of society.

It would seem that the new Jerusalem Temple, built by command of the Persians in about 515 BCE, was constructed hastily and without ornamentation. It was functional. By this stage any remaining outline of an earlier building, the so-called Temple of Solomon or First Temple as minutely described in Literary Israel, but destroyed by the Babylonians some seventy years earlier, would have been conjectural. We have no idea of the First Temple's footprint, nor what took place within its confines. However, the Second Temple was accepted as replacing an earlier magnificent Temple of Yahweh, only known to us by means of Literary Israel. Historically, we have only the slightest information about the earlier Temple.

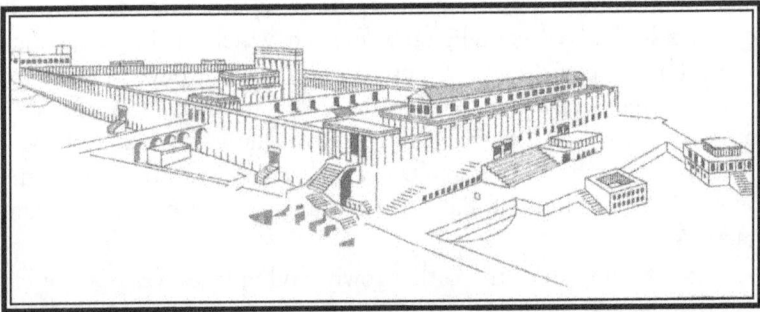

*Figure 3*
*Archaeological reconstruction of the Second Temple*
*as extended by Herod the Great*

In short, Persia had a strategic policy that included: first, resettling peoples in new locations; next, either the building or restoration of temples; thirdly, setting up a system of military defence, agriculture and administration; and finally, the establishment of law-codes considered to have been provided by the temple deity. Perhaps, in Yehud, by the end of the sixth century BCE, the economic and agricultural renewal was successfully underway, and this would have been followed by a military restructure in the mid-fifth century BCE. This renewal and restructuring would have been accompanied by some legal and constitutional establishment. The Law of Yahweh would have been compiled side by side with the economic and agricultural changes.

The new society, with its mixed population, would have been in a state of confusion. Persian political rule meant that any earlier social class system was defunct. There would have been noticeable social differences between the privileged newly-arrived immigrants (about 5% of the population), dispatched by the Persians, and the locals left there in Yehud by the Babylonian and Persian conquerors. There would have been tensions between these two strata of society, as well as between the very parochial culture of the one and a more cosmopolitan culture of the other, between urban dwellers and rural people, between those who accepted the High God Yahweh and those who still followed local cults (even perhaps that of the fertility form of the god, Yahweh). Yahweh the High God, as an unattached male with no consort and sole creator of the world, was more similar to the gods in the East – such as Sin (Akkadia), Marduk (Babylonia), Ahura Mazda (Persia) – than the fertility god, Yahweh, known in earlier times in the region.

The Persians, and the new immigrants themselves, both wanted the same thing: that the immigrants should take over the land as their own, and manage it efficiently for the benefit of their Persian overlords. The immigrants had come with funds to build a new Temple and to begin the process of indigenization. Their first step would have been to give priority to scribal activity. They needed to counter any presumption on the part of those left behind in the land that it was theirs, even though that presumption might well have had the most solid foundation. If this 'people of the land' (as they became known) wanted to be part of a new 'Israel', they must conform to a new definition of God, society and ethnicity.[8]

As the Persian political control became the order of the day, the following social institutions were set up, established on the basis of the new Temple: a priesthood, a sacrificial system, a caste system, a charter of holiness and a scribal centre. This is not to say that religion, as a separate entity, dominated. Politics and economics dominated; religion was enmeshed in them.

Court scribes, tutored in this environment, wrote a 'history' (in parentheses, as it would have been quite different from our idea of history) of Yehud, which created for it an identity that went back to an earlier 'Israel' and its antecedents. It would be better if we used the term Story instead of History. This Story would presumably have been based not only on the new Persian ideology but on some local living memories and traditions, and even some archival materials. In the main, though, in constructing their Story, the scribes followed the line of argument provided by their masters. The discourse explained the status of the community of that time, and verified the rights and privileges of the immigrant élite within that society. Into this new Story there were inserted Exile-like events in which an immigrant group takes over a land and rule its previous inhabitants: traditions regarding Abraham leaving Ur and coming to Canaan; traditions about a suffering group's Exodus out of Egypt (where they had been exiled by the Egyptians) and the Taking of the Land of Canaan by Joshua. These were cleverly combined and attributed to Yahweh. In each case the local existing inhabitants of the new land were described as 'the Canaanites', or as related ethnic groups.

In the case of the Abraham Story, the newly arrived group identified itself with the true Israel, descended from an Ancestor, the son of Abraham and Sarah – Isaac. The people of the land, depicted as the Canaanites, were descended from the other son of Abraham (but by the secondary wife, Hagar), Ishmael. In the case of the Moses Story the newly-arrived group consisted of the Twelve Tribes descended from Jacob, who was also called Israel.

This was the beginning, the first draft as it were, of Literary Israel. But it was not yet Literary Israel.

The existence of a scribal school presumes that the members had dedicated time, the resources, sufficient access to archives and motivation to write. They would have been professionals, paid and supported either by the Temple or by the Persian administration directly. The scribes were seen as an important part of the society; they did not write for leisure, there was purpose in their labour. Commercial records controlled the economy; archiving controlled the past or responded to antiquarian interests; 'history' or Story-writing recreated a preferred past that gave precedence to the newcomers; prophetic texts could critique both the past and the present as well as point to a future, without involving the writers in any responsibility; wisdom writing maintained the social status and mores of the élite; later, the new genre of apocalyptic writing would attempt to control the future.

This growing body of literature was very close to what we would know today in the Hebrew Scriptures, not complete though and not so organised. It would not have been what we like to call religious literature. The next phase would see the literature become Scripture.

Following the collapse of the Persian Empire, the Greeks moved eastwards and endeavoured to spread Hellenistic culture and religion in the Near East. The Judeans, the descendants from the mixed population of Yehud, retaliated by reinforcing their nationalism. Circumcision, the avoidance of pork and other dietary rules and the cult of the High God Yahweh became stabilising features. The written scrolls became part of both their culture and national identity. No longer were they a Persian creation; they belonged to the people of Judah.

At some time in the Greek period, the Hebrew scrolls underwent a great change in understanding and authority. They became the sacred symbol of a people and its culture and its religion. One text from the collection could be used to interpret another; texts from the past could be used to scrutinise the future. Certain teacher-figures in the community could be trusted to interpret the texts. There had been a move away from the scrolls as controlling nationalistic history to scrolls being themselves divine and everlasting truth, controlling a religious life. This was the beginning of Literary Israel as a separate sacred item. We can now speak of the Hebrew Scriptures, the Bible, as the receptacle of Literary Israel.

Now comes the big question: when can these dramatic developments bringing about Literary Israel, be placed in an historical sequence? The only answer that allows any credibility is – the time of the Hasmonean dynasty. It is necessary to understand more clearly the identity of the Hasmoneans.

### The Hasmoneans

We can never be sure of the historical details, but the later Jewish tradition related that in a rural area the simmering local revolt against the foreign Greeks ignited in the early second century BCE. According to a tradition, it was in Modein, a town north west of Jerusalem, that a village priest called Mattathias refused to offer a pig-sacrifice to Zeus when so ordered. A bystander offered to sacrifice in his stead, and Mattathias killed both the renegade and the Syrian commander. Then Mattathias, his five sons and some loyal followers fled into the wilderness. From there they waged guerrilla warfare on the Greeks.

Mattathias died soon after but he was succeeded by his eldest son, Judas, known as *Maccabeus*.[9] Father and son were regarded as the eponymous heads of a line that would become known as the Hasmoneans, probably because Mattathias' grandfather had been named Asamonaeus. Within that Hasmonean house, Judas and his four brothers would become known as The Maccabees. Filled with religious zeal, Judas and his growing group of local discontents managed to defeat rather dispirited Greek forces. They soon retook Jerusalem and demolished the Greek altar set up by the Greek king and restored the Temple to Yahweh and his ritual. This cleansing of the Temple was to be commemorated by the establishment of a feast called *Hanukkah* or Feast of Dedication.

The Hasmoneans would remain in place almost to the Christian period, until the Romans arrived with their mighty military force. In the meantime, the Hasmonean State saw itself as the successor to David and Solomon as described in the scrolls, the fulfilment of all that the people of Judah had sought. This state adopted the Hebrew Scriptures, the Story and its accompaniments composed under the Persians and then inserted their own order into the stories.

It is only at this point that we can talk about Judaism as a religion. It was the official religion of the Hasmoneans. Its charter text was the Hebrew Scriptures, originally produced by the scribes attached to the Temple built under Persian control. These writings were seen by the Hasmoneans as a sacred phenomenon produced under the control of Yahweh. The focal point of Judaism was the Temple, built by the Persians it was true, but now it was a Hasmonean possession. This Story was that of Literary Israel.

The scrolls were edited so as to include an overall chronology of dates to show clearly that the cleansing of the Temple event was the high-point of all human history. The Hasmoneans saw themselves as the fulfilment of Literary Israel.

By simply counting the figures given in the biblical text, the period from creation until the Exodus from Egypt is 2666 years. This is two-thirds of 4000 years, a period regarded as a world epoch in the thinking of that time. The coincidence is obvious. This full cycle of 4000 years would end with the re-dedication of the Temple under Judas Maccabeus in 164 BCE:

**Creation → Exodus: 2666 years**
**Creation → Re-dedication of Temple: 4000 years**

Within these parameters the Jewish Story was given its own chronology:

Exodus → Building of First Temple: 480 years
Building of First Temple → Building of Second Temple: 480 years

Why 480? Probably it was the sum of 12 (for the Twelve Tribes) multiplied by the universal number of 40. However, we may never clearly understand the system on which the biblical dates have been based. It is sufficient to say that they were not intended to be historical reference points; they are symbolic numbers inserted under Hasmonean authority.

We have now arrived in this review to the cusp of the millennium. Judaism was seen at this time as the religion of the Judean people who resisted the Greeks. Just as the immigrants had established a Story to give themselves validity, so did the Hasmoneans; they adapted the earlier Story composed under the Persians. The Story would outlive them all. It was the Story of a suffering people who were led by their treaty with the High God, Yahweh, and who found a Land which they could inhabit in peaceful security. It was a Good Land. There, these once downtrodden people could be themselves and find fulfilment in a Kingdom of God.

Like all religions, Judaism required a succession. Literary Israel provided the great moment when contact was made with the God of Israel, Yahweh. It involved the Moses story:

**Focus on Ultimacy: The High God Yahweh**

↓

**Other-worldly Intermediaries: Word of Yahweh, the Spirit of Yahweh, the Angel of Yahweh**

**(Contact Achieved)**

**This-worldly Intermediary: 'Moses'**

↑

**Religious Group at Sinai**

This was the moment of contact. How could this moment be replicated? 'Moses' had to have successors. So Moses (whose story had been foreshadowed in the Abraham story) handed on his role to Joshua, the hero of yet another story of new conquest. From Joshua there came the Judges and these morphed into the Kings and also Prophets like Elijah and Elisha. After the Second Temple was established the role of the High Priest became a Moses-like role and certainly the Hasmonean kings, who took over the High Priesthood, saw themselves as successors to Moses. Finally, the Hebrew Scriptures themselves, with their wondrous events and profound thoughts became the Intermediary. The big question was: who is Moses today? Or again: is Moses to come in the future as another Prophet, a Messiah or some other God-sent being?

By the time of Jesus of Nazareth there were many claimants to the role of 'Moses' within the Judaism of the time: the written Scripture, the Priest-Kings, various Prophets.

*The study of 'Israel' raises the vital question of Literary Israel, Historical Israel and Biblical Israel. Literary Israel is the focus of religious study and the most important of the three from our point of view, being interested as we are primarily in religious things. Historical Israel is fascinating, but it is the domain of historians and archaeologists who endeavour to explain the seemingly random events of the past.*

*Biblical Israel should be consigned to the extinction bin.*

*Literary Israel began as the statement of national identity, created from previous sources by the scribes of the Persian satrapy of Yehud. As time passed, it became accepted as the Story of the populace of Judah. Under the Hasmoneans it was transformed into a Sacred Story. It was used not as a statement about the past, a justification for land settlement, but as a sacred book that guided people in the present.*

*Literary Israel, as it reads today and as it was read by early Christian times, was a statement that God's people, despite setback and persecution, would find fulfilment in the Kingdom of God, the Reign of God on earth. The people would be able to contact the God of Israel through certain structures. This contact had been originally achieved by Moses and then other leaders down to the Hasmonean Priest-Kings. These Priest-Kings were This-worldly Intermediaries.*

*The Other-worldly Intermediaries, sent from Yahweh, took many forms. The earliest were the Cloud and the Tower of Fire described during the Exodus story, but later there were the Word of Yahweh and the Spirit of Yahweh. As the fortunes of the people declined they despaired of the present and looked to the future for an Intermediary. One day, they claimed, there would be a great revival and a Just One, a Prophet, a Son of God (not divine), a Messiah (or Christ, an 'anointed' person like the kings of old) would be sent to function as the Intermediary. In short, someone would surely come to be their Intermediary.*

*What we now want to see is how, from Literary Israel, there developed first, a Literary Jesus based on an Historical Jesus, and next a number of Jesus-movements and finally the writing of the Christian Scriptures and the Roman Church with its Papal leadership. We also want to see how all of these fitted together.*

# NOTES

Some of this material and various other general matters pertaining to the Hebrew Scriptures and the Christian Scriptures have been published in a different form in my book (1996), *The Jesus Question. The Historical Search*, HarperCollins Religious: Melbourne. Other materials pertaining to both the Hebrew Scriptures and Christian Scriptures were covered in my subsequent book (2003). *Beyond the Jesus Question. Confronting the Historical Jesus*, PostPressed: Flaxton, Qld. I have further expanded on these books in another book already mentioned: (2012), *Three Revolutions. Three Drastic Changes in Interpreting the Bible*, ATF Press: Hindmarsh.

Material from these books have been used in different contexts in this present book and I do not make tedious references.

On the study of ancient Israel relevant to the approach above, see:

Davies, Philip (1992), *In Search of 'Ancient Israel'*, Sheffield Academic Press: London and New York

Davies, Philip (1998), *Scribes and Schools. The Canonization of the Hebrew Scriptures*, Westminster John Knox Press: Louisville

Finkelstein, I. and Silberman, N. (2001), *The Bible Unearthed: Archaeology's New Vision of Ancient Israel and the Origin of its Sacred Texts*, The Free Press: New York and London

Marcus, A. (2000), *Rewriting the Bible: How Archaeology is Reshaping the Middle East*, Little, Brown and Company: London

Thompson, Thomas (2000), *The Bible in History. How writers create a past*, Pimlico: London

Levine, A-J. et al., eds. (2006), *The Historical Jesus in Context*, Princeton University Press: Princeton and Oxford.

# 2/
# THE JESUS STORY –
# LITERARY JESUS

*Hopefully we now have a clear understanding of Literary Israel. Literary Israel described the social and cultural world into which the Historical Jesus of Nazareth was born.*

*As was the case with the study of Israel, a terminology similar to that used in discussing the Hebrew Scriptures can be applied to more recent interpretations of the Christian Scriptures or the New Testament.*[10] *This new interpretation has been stimulated by advances in scholarship: new literary methods of interpretation, the rethinking that has taken place as a result of the discovery of the Dead Sea Scrolls and the Gnostic texts from the Egyptian desert at Nag Hammadi and also the application of sciences such as anthropology and sociology to the biblical tradition.*[11]

*The terminology I have devised relates to a Literary Jesus, an Historical Jesus and a Biblical Jesus.*

*Literary Israel can explain how the Literary Jesus came to be and explain the contexts and understandings within that Story. From the Literary Jesus we can move to a new Story, the Story of the Church. This is simply an extension of the Literary Jesus Story into the future.*

*One more item of terminology needs to be explained – the Jesus-movement. The 'Jesus-movement' began immediately after the death of Jesus. Stirred by the activity of the Historical Jesus there were groups of Jews who followed his stimulus. They were multiform and different. At this stage it is far too early to talk about a 'Christian' Church; the Jesus-movements were still part of Judaism.*

From the outset, it should be made clear that there was certainly an Historical Jesus, a person whom historians can identify in the early part of the first millennium CE. The Literary Jesus is the Story of a Jesus as it is contained in the Christian Scriptures, almost exclusively the four gospels. The Biblical Jesus is the insertion of the Historical Jesus into the Literary Jesus. Like Biblical Israel, it has produced a hybrid that never existed and has no purpose.

We begin with the Literary Jesus.

### Literary Jesus

The Literary Jesus is the Jesus of the gospels. In fact, there are four Literary Jesus-es in the canonical gospels. They have their own versions of the Story (admittedly with significant overlaps) and they have their own line of argument. We have no idea regarding the authorship of the four canonical gospels and can only date them with hesitation. However, we will continue to use the traditional names of Matthew, Mark, Luke and John for convenience. These names were not commonly applied to the four gospels until the second century CE.

We will take the Literary Jesus in Mark's gospel as an example. The gospel can be structured as follows in order to present Mark's Literary Jesus:

Prologue 1:1-13
John the Baptist – the one who announces Jesus' coming
Jesus is baptised as the Messiah
Jesus begins a battle with Satan
A. 1:14-8:30
Mark shows by means of stories, sayings and disputes that

Jesus is the Messiah

A Blind Man is healed.

The first disciples confess: 'You are the Messiah!'

B. 8:31-10:52

Mark shows that following Jesus the Messiah entails suffering and self-giving

A Blind Man is healed

The first disciples decide to follow the Messiah to Jerusalem

C. 11:1-16:8

Mark describes the death and resurrection of the Messiah

(End of gospel probably missing)

The Prologue identifies Jesus as the Messiah, succeeding to the prophet-like John the Baptist, a most austere man of the desert, who had come to confront evil in the world and save his Jewish brethren from the end of times. As mentioned earlier, Messiah means the 'Anointed One' in Hebrew. There was a variety of expectations about an Anointed One who would come to save the Jews. Some thought that the Messiah would be belligerent; others thought he would be peaceful; some thought there would be one; others thought there would be two or more. Jews would not have considered the Messiah to be divine. The Prologue then describes a final battle between Jesus and Satan (the leader of evil demons) that takes place in a desert. This sets the context for the role of Jesus as Messiah. He has come to conquer evil.

Mark describes the ministry of the Messiah in Galilee in the first section, marked as above. Jesus performs the works expected of a Messiah: he gathers followers and makes them into a 'Twelve', a New Israel; he teaches, heals and debates with religious opponents in the manner expected of the Messiah and finally he is met consistently with hostility and rejection. The Literary Jesus calls for The Twelve to make an affirmation of faith in him as the Messiah. The disciples make the affirmation through Peter.

In the second section, B above, Jesus and these disciples make a final journey to Jerusalem where, in section C, he fulfills the role of the Messiah by dying and rising from the dead.

A key part of the Literary Jesus story in Mark is the account of Jesus' selection of disciples. The gospel relates, as part of the closely knit story, that a group of disciples who had been called from their everyday occupations, had then been formed into a 'Twelve' reflecting a revitalised Israel and finally sent on a mission to continue the messianic task of Jesus. The Twelve are unsure, lacking confidence. Then Jesus cures a blind man. It has its effect; at the centre of the gospel they finally come to faith. Jesus prepares them to accompany him on what is called The Way. This is no ordinary journey; it will lead to Jerusalem, the hub of the world, the place where history is to come to its high-point with the death and resurrection of the Messiah. Before they can confront this last stage another blind man is cured. The repeated cure of a blind man is one of the rhetorical devices included in the Markan story. We will see that the choice of The Twelve, of whom Peter is designated leader, is most important in this version.

Mark would seem to be the first written gospel in the canon, dating from about 65 CE, some thirty years after the death of Jesus. Whether that 65 CE gospel was exactly the same as the gospel we have today is unlikely.

Matthew would have been written within the next ten years, around the same time as Luke. His gospel used some form of Mark's gospel and also a collection of sayings and stories attributed to Jesus (which was not in Mark). Luke also used Mark and this same collection of sayings and stories, although he put them into different contexts than Matthew and made his own additions.

Scholars have referred to this collection of sayings and stories, the overlap in Matthew and Luke which does not occur in Mark, as 'Q', which is short for Quelle, German for 'source'. Today, many prefer to use the title 'Sayings Gospel Q'. There is evidence that this was a separate gospel (even though no separate manuscript has ever been found), used by Church members even prior to the time of the four canonical gospels. In the Sayings Gospel Q, Jesus appears as a healer and exorcist in Galilee. What he is achieving by clearing the world of demons, and their impact on sickness and ignorance, is the Kingdom of God or the Reign of God. This is a worldly haven where the inhabitants have accepted the principles of Yahweh, the God of Israel. There is safety therein. Jesus promises that in these new times safety and food will be readily available for those who trust God.

However, only the Jews are regarded as being part of this promise. Jesus shows that he is continuing in the path of his onetime leader, John the Baptist, but he is more relaxed and more open and gentle. Because of the contrast with John, he is criticised for being a welcoming host to all classes of people, including sinners, and for meeting with these people over table meals and indulging in alcohol.

Who would have composed and used the Sayings Gospel Q? Most probably some of the very early Jesus groups after the death of Jesus who still expected their movement to remain within Judaism. They were Jews and they had not yet realised that others, also motivated by Jesus, were focussing on a mission to the outsiders, the Gentiles. At a later date some of these groups became known as Ebionites ('The Poor') and they were rejected by both Jews and those Christians who had extended their mission into the Gentile world. This would explain why the first of the Beatitudes (part of the Sayings Gospel Q) begins in Matthew: Blessed are the Poor!

The Sayings Gospel Q cannot be considered a transcript of what Jesus may have said or preached. It would have been a remembered collection of texts, undoubtedly undergoing editing and pruning as time went on. However, it would have been earlier than the four canonical gospels.

This is the text that Matthew adopted and combined with his version of Mark. Matthew was commissioned by a community that included Gentiles but was still within the Palestinian area. Gradually it became the most popular gospel and its text became known as far as Egypt and was extensively used by early Christian scholars.

Based on Mark and the Sayings Gospel Q, Matthew formulated his own Literary Jesus. This Jesus is presented as a Moses-like Messiah in a highly structured writing which follows that of Mark but makes significant changes to allow for the insertion of material from the Sayings Gospel Q.

Thus, Matthew's gospel begins with a Jesus infancy-narrative peppered with references to Moses taken from the Hebrew Scriptures. Jesus is given the sacred name of Immanuel (Hebrew for 'God with Us'). Jesus' public ministry in Matthew, reusing the material from Mark and also from Sayings Gospel Q, is divided into five books of Stories/Sayings, parallel to the Five Books of Moses in the Hebrew Scriptures. The Five Books culminate with the ministry of Jesus in Jerusalem and the account of his death, more or less parallel with what Matthew would have received from his source – Mark. His death is the death of a suffering Messiah.

Matthew's resurrection consists of the combination of a Vision from Jesus, returned from the dead in Galilee, and the story of the empty tomb in Jerusalem. Jesus' final exhortation is: 'I am with you'. It corresponds to the title of Immanuel used, as we have seen, as the sacred name for Jesus in the opening infancy-narrative and intended to form an inclusio, a connection between the beginning of the gospel and its end.

Luke's gospel also combines Mark and the Sayings Gospel Q. Its structure is continued into Luke's second volume, the Acts of the Apostles. The Literary Jesus of Luke's gospel is, as with Matthew and Luke, a Messiah, but Luke has depicted his Messiah-Jesus in the manner of a prophet announcing that the End Times are near.

The Prophet-Messiah prepares the first stage of his ministry in Galilee. Then the gospel describes a remarkable and extensive journey to Jerusalem, replete with sayings, stories and good works (mostly taken from the Sayings Gospel Q). It covers some ten of Luke's twenty-four chapters in length, a veritable travelogue. At the culmination of the journey Jesus reaches Jerusalem, where he is rejected by mainstream Judaism and condemned to death.

Tellingly, as Jesus dies on the cross in Luke's gospel, a Gentile centurion announces: 'Truly this man was a Just One'. The Literary Jesus is interpreted as a Just One (in Hebrew, a zaddik). Among the Jews, the Just Ones were thought to be holy men who lived ascetic lives. They intervened on the part of the people and every generation needed one or more of them. They were able to pray for the people to God in hard times, to protect them, to heal their ills. For particular groups, a Just One could become their This-worldly Intermediary.

Luke has a more extended resurrection section with appearances to women, then to two disciples on the road to Emmaus and finally to the group of disciples. The gospel concludes with an Ascension into Heaven story.

However, in order to appreciate Luke's full message, the Acts of the Apostles should be read as the second volume of his great opus. It shows how the disciples, having been instructed and prepared by Jesus during his lifetime, in turn continue to spread God's new message. Jesus is physically with the disciples at first and they are filled with the Spirit of God, God's powerful presence. Repeating the earlier story of the Ascension in Acts, the Literary Jesus of Luke appears to the disciples and says:

> It is not for you to know the times or periods that the Father has set by his own authority. But you will receive power when the Holy Spirit has come upon you; and you will be my witnesses in Jerusalem, in all Judaea and Samaria, and to the ends of the earth. (Acts 1:7-8)

This is the divine plan which is clearly stated, immediately after the events of the Gospel of Luke. It is a much more extensive plan than in the Sayings Gospel Q, which was restricted to the people of Israel and the establishment of their Reign of God in their midst. The Acts begins its Church Story in Jerusalem, where wondrous things occur through the ministry of The Twelve with Peter at their head. They are similar to the great things done by Jesus himself earlier. Then the disciples move outwards first into Judaea and Samaria and thence, through the ministry of Paul, to Asia Minor and Europe, 'the ends of the earth'. What had begun with Jesus among the Jews had now spread beyond Israel to the whole world.

Matthew, Mark and Luke – they are called the 'Synoptics', since their gospels describe Jesus from a similar perspective – had substantially the same Literary Jesus, but with some important variations. In each case Jesus was the Just One and Messiah, but the experience of the group associated with a particular gospel must have coloured the presentation of each of these Literary Jesus-es.

The Literary Jesus in John's gospel is presented quite differently to the other three canonical gospels. He is a clearly a divine, ethereal being, the Word of God, who is quietly aware of all that is taking place. This Word took on a human form. The gospel was written much later than the others, after 100 CE and much later than the time of the Historical Jesus.

In the opening Hymn in John chapter 1, the Son is depicted as a heavenly being who subsequently took on the human form of Jesus. This Literary Jesus would later return to the divine realm. To understand the public ministry of this Literary Jesus (depicted quite differently to the Synoptics), it is necessary to understand what was meant when John used the terminology of 'signs' a number of times in order to present the activity of this Messiah in his gospel.

A 'sign' in John is a human activity in which the Literary Jesus reveals his true purpose, mission and identity. As it presently stands, the first 'sign' is changing water (intended for Jewish ablutions) into wine at the wedding feast of Cana. Jesus' action shows that the old order of Judaism (the water) is being replaced by a new order of Christianity (the wine of Messianic times). There are seven of these 'signs', the final one being at the Cross on Golgotha. The astute reader is led inexorably from one to the next and expected to deepen in faith as the plot progresses. Between the signs, there are Discourses, later additions and corrections inserted by editors. By the gospel's conclusion the reader should be able to believe that Jesus is the Son of God. This is a tightly-knit, complex text that requires much analysis.

The Gospel of John insists that it is the Literary Jesus who reveals the divine Son of God, the Word. This revelation is what is ultimately important, not the human actions of an Historical Jesus. This is definitively explained in John's resurrection story. It states that just as the Historical Jesus of Galilee was once a This-worldly Intermediary for a restricted group of Jewish followers who lived side by side with him, so the Literary Jesus, identified from the Hebrew Scriptures and proclaimed by the preaching of the believing group, acts as an Intermediary for all later believers. John's Literary Jesus is 'another Paraclete' or Intermediary, the 'Spirit of Truth' or the one who leads disciples to understand the deepest purposes of The Father. This latter 'Jesus' is the important factor, not the historical Jesus of Galilee. Hence, the meaning of two well-known Johannine texts becomes clearer: first that spoken to Mary Magdalene:

Do not continue to hold on to me, because I have not yet
ascended to the Father. (20:17)

and that spoken to Thomas:

Blessed are those who have not seen and yet have come to believe'.
(20: 29)

The message is clear: access to the Literary Jesus, via the Scriptures and preaching, is the way to salvation for all peoples. No one is saved today by an Historical Jesus.

John's gospel ends in this way:

Now Jesus did many other signs **(Note: 'signs' are human actions of Jesus that reveal a divine message and his identity to an audience)** in the presence of his disciples, which are not written in this book **(Note: don't worry about other 'events' attributed to Jesus; you only need the ones in this book).** But these are written so that you may come to believe that Jesus is the Messiah **(Note: 'Messiah' is the leader sent by God),** the Son of God **(Note: for Jews this first meant a human very close to God and his purposes; it later acquired, as here, the meaning of a divine being),** and that through believing you may have life **(Note: this 'life' is the fullness of life, the deepest characteristic of being truly human)** in his name **(Note: 'name' implies the special God-given power of this Literary Jesus).** (20:30-31)

In other words, John is requiring his audience to read or listen to the Signs of the Literary Jesus in his gospel, come to 'Truth' (the saving knowledge of God bestowed on humans who read the Signs correctly) and to have their lives transformed by doing so.[12]

In each of the four canonical gospels, the Literary Jesus is variously depicted as the Just One, the Messiah and the Son of God. The Just One, in Judaism a holy man who represents the people, has been overlaid by the Synoptics with the trappings of the Moses-like Messiah and a David-like Messiah, as described by some Jews of the time. By the time of John, Jesus has acquired divine features from the beginning. This means that within the four gospels a complex description of Jesus had been expanded with elements taken from the stories of Moses, Joshua, David, Elijah and Elisha recited in Literary Israel as well as the statements concerning Yahweh as the Word and the Spirit.

Peter is prominent in the Story of Literary Jesus, much more so in the Synoptics than John. We have already seen that the central point of Mark's gospel was the statement of faith by Peter: 'You are the Messiah!' In Mark and Luke, Jesus does not continue or extend the conversation. However, the Gospel of Matthew expanded the text so that Jesus responds:

Blessed are you Simon bar-Jona. For flesh and blood has not revealed this to you, but my Father who is in heaven. And I tell you, you are Peter, and on this rock I will build my church, and the powers of death shall not prevail against it. I will give you the keys of the kingdom of heaven, and whatever you bind on earth shall be bound in heaven, and whatever you loose on earth shall be loosed in heaven. (16:17-18)

This is a theological commentary, produced long after the time of the Historical Jesus and reflecting the beliefs of a group who had developed far from their roots in the Jesus-movement. Matthew has inserted it into his gospel. These are not the words of the Historical Jesus but of the Literary Jesus of Matthew. The text will become very important for the later Church Story.

In John, Peter is present but his prominence is muted. He has competitors such as The Beloved Disciple and Mary Magdalene. We will come back to this important point.

The Literary Jesus makes it clear that Jesus contacted God. This was the God of Israel, Yahweh. However, the experience is now changed, transformed. Jesus has replaced Moses, the kings, the prophets, the

Hasmonean Priest-kings. His new focus is not Yahweh but something radically changed, *'abba* (perhaps something like 'Daddy' in Aramaic), Father (*pater*, in Greek). Jesus is linked to The Father.

We can now turn to the Historical Jesus, the history of Jesus that can be constructed from historical sources by the historical method.

### The Historical Jesus

What do we know historically of Jesus? Rather little. The following is a synopsis using narrative texts and sayings taken from the four canonical gospels (since there are virtually no other historical records concerning Jesus) with historical discrimination and due suspicion, certainly not accepting that the four gospels were intended to be historical records in the first place, accepting more readily those narrative descriptions and sayings which are recorded by more than one independent writer and which do not betray any obvious theological bias or intent. What follows readily accepts what we know of the historical context in which Jesus would have lived, particularly as described in the writings of Flavius Josephus[13] and archaeological reports. No detailed substantiation of the 'events' is offered.[14]

Jesus of Nazareth would have been born between 6 and 4 BCE. He probably came from the obscure township of Nazareth, the first mention of which is in an inscription from Caesarea only written in the fourth century CE. Presumably he was born there.

Only Matthew and Luke mention his birth in Bethlehem and their theological motive is only too clear – to prop up the messianic claim that he was of Davidic lineage since David's origins were in Bethlehem. They narrate contradictory stories. In Luke, Jesus' family travelled to Bethlehem from Nazareth on account of an historically unattested census. Therefore, he was born in Bethlehem, although he was known as 'Jesus of Nazareth'. In Matthew, the family lived in Bethlehem prior to Jesus' birth and only settled in Nazareth after they returned from a flight to Egypt,[15] and that is why he was known as 'Jesus of Nazareth'. Mark, the earliest gospel, relates nothing concerning Jesus' pre-adult life, while John seems to indicate that there was no unanimous belief among his contemporaries about Jesus being born in Bethlehem.

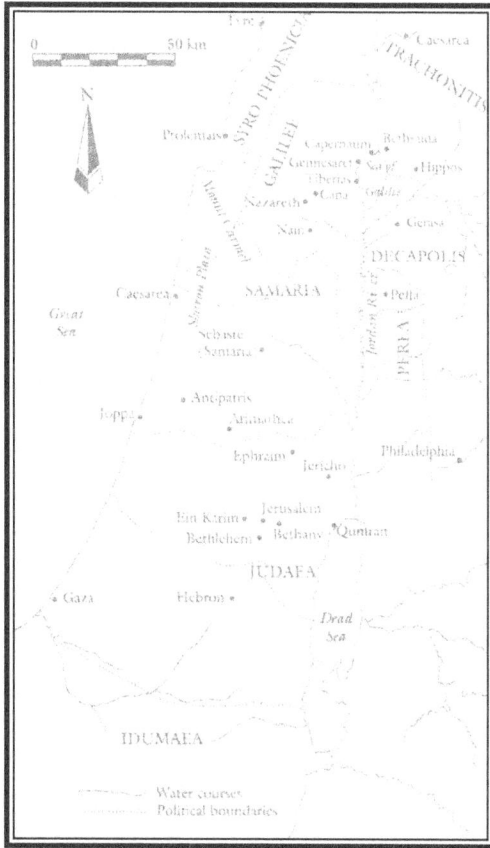

*Figure 4*
*Palestine in the first century CE*

The virginal conception of Jesus is affirmed only in Matthew and Luke. It is 'proved' by the misinterpretation of the text of Isaiah 7:14: 'Therefore Yahweh himself will give you a sign. Look, the young woman (*'alma*) is with child and shall bear a son, and shall name him Immanuel.' The Hebrew *'alma* or 'young woman' (probably a reference to the pregnancy of one of King Hezekiah's wives) had been mistranslated in the Greek rendition of the Hebrew Scriptures (the Septuagint, the text usually used by learned early Christians) by the Greek *parthenos* or 'physical virgin'. The resultant reading ('A Virgin shall conceive') was transformed into a theological statement, valuable as a Christian affirmation of the unique importance of Jesus, but not an historical fact or a biological marvel. Most probably, some Jews expected that the unfulfilled prophecy of one born of a Virgin would be fulfilled by the Messiah, and since Jesus was later identified as the Messiah the prophecy was applied to him. The likelihood is that Jesus was the natural son of Mary and Joseph, having four brothers and some sisters, all of them born in Nazareth.

It is claimed in a gospel text that Jesus was by occupation a *tekton*, like his father, a relatively unusual term which described someone in the broad semi-skilled category of a carpenter, a stonemason or a smithy. There does not seem to have been any theological reason why this occupation would have been concocted. Most probably, it indicated that his predecessors had been dispossessed of land and consequently he belonged to a lower social stratum in Galilee.

The first event that can be reliably attributed to the Historical Jesus is his baptism by John when he was already a mature man. This is clearly treated with such embarrassed circumspection by the four canonical evangelists (John's gospel makes it clear that he was *not* baptised by the Baptist) that it could hardly have been a theological invention. John the Baptist was a charismatic prophetic type whose baptism of his followers in the waters of the Jordan was a ritual identifying those who were prepared to meet the coming Messianic Era. The ritual baptism was an acting-out of the crossing of the Jordan by the Israelites in the Book of Joshua, itself a replication of the crossing of the Sea of Reeds by the Exodus generation in the book of Exodus. Those who participated in the ritual would have emerged from the river water and entered a symbolically new Promised Land, the Kingdom or Reign of God, a sacred space at a sacred time. John was a prophet of doom, foretelling the imminent closure of the present order of things prior to this transformation. The historian Josephus tells of other Jewish prophets around this time who had a similar ritual and a similar message.

While Jesus doubtless might have found a temporary niche in John's following and would have been stimulated by John's anti-establishment rhetoric, his own calling was to take a different turn. At some point in time, Jesus moved away from and abandoned John. John was the fierce ascetic, living in the desert as a prophetic figure, catering for other extremists; Jesus was more interested in the everyday populace of Galilee and their daily needs.

Considering the evidence, it would seem that Jesus was recognised in his Galilean setting at the time as a *zaddik*, a Just One, a local Jewish saint. This is a title we have already encountered. As such his ministry in Galilee can be explained: he healed, cast out demons, used his wit against the errors of his opponents (there was a close link between these activities;

they were all caused by demonic activity, something taken for granted in those times). By so doing, he announced the coming Reign of God, a social world where Jews could live their lives in safety and peace. The details of time, place and specific activities related to his ministry cannot be reconstructed. The gospel stories are not historical and we have no other sources.

Linked with this ministry Jesus promoted table fellowship. His communal meals were open to all, including the locals but also women, even prostitutes, public sinners and the tax-collectors.[16] This Jesus-following comprised the common folk, the outcasts of society, the marginalised, to whom Jesus offered entry into the Reign of God by means of his table fellowship, outside the normal ritual channels of Judaism.

In short, slowly but surely the Reign of God was being established for the Jewish people in Galilee by Jesus' ministry.

In either 30 or 33 CE, Jesus the Just One, having established a Galilean following (which would seem to have included women, and particularly a rich woman called Mary from Magdala), went on a pilgrimage to Jerusalem for the celebration of Passover. It may have been his sole journey to the holy city; certainly, he was not an habitual visitor. Dismayed at the display of commerce and political power in the Temple, he was involved in some sort of demonstration by which he expressed his concern over the rank worldliness of the Temple cult. For causing this disturbance he was arrested. Jerusalem, at festival time, was a tinder-box, waiting for just one disruptive spark. While Jesus might have been allowed to strike sparks in Galilee with audacity, the Roman authorities would not allow him to do so in Jerusalem at Passover.

Thereafter, the four gospels are replete with contradictions and inconsistencies concerning his arrest, trial, condemnation and death. It is difficult to sift the details. What seems to be historically reliable is that he was arrested by Romans, perhaps with the collusion of some Jewish authorities, on the charge of causing insurrection against the Roman rule and executed. The final legal responsibility for the charge against him, his condemnation and his crucifixion rested with Rome.

Whether Pilate would have been involved directly, in what would have been a rather mundane administrative process of executing an insurrectionist, is also questionable. By the time the gospels were written the formula was fixed: 'Jesus died when Pontius Pilate was Prefect'; the Literary Jesus died charged as 'Jesus of Nazareth, King of the Jews'. This meant neither more nor less than that Jesus had died at the hand of

Roman imperial authority on the charge of incitement to insurrection. Pilate could well have been brought into the gospel tradition at a much later date.

Nor is there sufficient historical reason to explain why the Jewish Sanhedrin should have been involved. By the time of the written gospels, there had been a growing tendency to place the blame for Jesus' death not on the Romans but on the Jewish authorities. Also, Christians wanted to exonerate Jesus from any civil charge that raised questions about his righteousness in Gentile circles. Any civil offence was excised from the tradition. The charge of insurrection would have been replaced by one of blasphemy. It would have been at this stage that Caiaphas, current High Priest at that time, and his powerful father-in-law, Annas, were introduced into the narrative, with stories of two meetings of a Sanhedrin court, replete with inconsistencies about their timing, about the charges laid against Jesus and about the outcomes of the trials. Pilate, in this exercise, was described as a vacillating Roman judge, offering to release Jesus and washing his hands of responsibility for his death, before he caved in to Jewish demands for Jesus' execution.

It seems that we have no solid historical knowledge about the involvement of Pilate in the trial of Jesus and should look with scepticism on the gospels' description of a 'trial' before Annas and Caiaphas. All three would certainly have been historical characters of that time but drawn into a fictive narrative that was designed for a theological purpose. Even more so, Luke's account of Jesus being sent by Pilate to Herod the Tetrarch should be looked on with scepticism.

It is clear that the gospel writers knew virtually nothing of the circumstances of the actual death of Jesus apart from the brute fact of his crucifixion. The various 'last words' spoken from the cross, his being offered vinegar, the division of his garments by lot, his mockery by Jewish authorities are not historical. They are borrowed from descriptions of the suffering of the Just One, especially as related in Psalms 22 and 69 and Isaiah 53 in the Hebrew Scriptures.

Jesus died by the Roman form of execution. That is about the sum of our knowledge relating to the death of the Historical Jesus.

The final narrative in the canonical gospels is the resurrection of Jesus from his tomb. It needs to be stated unequivocally that the resurrection statement – 'Jesus is risen from the dead' – is theological; it belongs to the Literary Jesus. It was never an historical event. As a tradition that was created sometime in the first century CE, its development can be reconstructed hypothetically.

The tradition originated with a number of Vision Stories. Jesus, who had gone to the sleep of the Just in *she'ol*, the Hebrew term for the abode of the sleeping dead, was said to have appeared in Visions to a select few of his followers. The Visions were not sporadic nor without purpose. A Vision was intended to indicate succession among Jesus' followers and to ensure that the Jesus-movement would continue beyond his death. There were many claimants to a Vision. Peter claimed that Jesus had appeared to him; James, who was called the 'Brother of the Lord', also claimed that Jesus had appeared to him during a meal; two men on a trip to Emmaus claimed that Jesus had appeared to them as they ate; Jesus appeared to a group of disciples including Peter by the Sea of Galilee and ate a fish breakfast with them; he appeared to women. One interesting context for some Visions was made clear – Jesus appeared at meals, at the table fellowship which had been the hallmark of his Galilean ministry.

After Jesus' death, designated leaders of the Jesus-movement, in competition with each other, continued to hold communal meals in his memory. The participants were convinced that Jesus was present at the meals, just as he had been at the summation of all table fellowship meals, the Last Supper held on the night before he died. There are many discrepancies about this Supper in the Synoptics and John. A legitimate conclusion is that the Supper belongs to the Literary Jesus. It was not an historical event.

But another tradition was adding a new dimension to the Jesus-Visions. This was increasing apocalypticism, the depiction of the final events that would soon bring the world-order to an end. Jesus' thinking in the Sayings Gospel Q had not included any reference to such a dramatic end of the world. His sayings and stories were more interested in the present, in setting up the Reign of God straightaway in the here and now. But, with his death, his followers became more apocalyptically-minded, drawing on details from Literary Israel. This expectation of the Coming End was written back into some Jesus-sayings. Apocalyptic thought had looked forward to the day when the dead would rise and the tombs would open. Jesus' tomb, it was then said, had been opened as the first-fruits of the general resurrection of all the just ones. This empty tomb tradition was linked to the earlier Jesus-visions: Jesus had risen from the tomb and appeared to one or more of his chosen ones and his empty tomb had been examined.

We are left with the identification of the Historical Jesus by his contemporaries as the Just One, and as also the Messiah and Son of God (not necessarily divine, but a Godly-man) by later followers after his death. In other words, he was first identified as a local saint, a Just One, in rural Galilee, an advocate of the people before their God. He was dedicated to the overturn of evil. As an individual Just One, his ministry of healing, of miracle working and table fellowship was a prolonged ritual that dramatised as well as effected God's progressive victory over the forces of evil. Evil was being conquered and human barriers were being dismantled. The Reign of God in the world was imminent.

Jesus wanted to revitalise the local Galilean community, to restore the values of a way of life fully in tune with the ideals of an ideal Judaism and to bring about for them the Reign of God. There is no evidence that he claimed the title of Messiah or the title of Son of God in the sense of being divine. He had no intention of moving out of Judaism, of founding another Church. He probably did not foresee that he would have a successor or needed one. For him, any succession would be in the hands of Yahweh, who designated Just Ones.

Later generations of his followers and gospel-writers would certainly interpret him as the Messiah of Israel and as the divine Son of God, although the two do not need to go together. This interpretation, written into the canonical gospels and affecting the choice and description of events and sayings, renders those writings almost useless for reliable historical research.

## The Biblical Jesus

Scholars dedicated to the Biblical Jesus insert the findings about the Historical Jesus into the stories of the Literary Jesus. Most proponents would maintain that they are thereby presenting another and better, more expansive, Historical Jesus. They are not. They are mixing Story and History, Literary Jesus and Historical Jesus, in a highly inappropriate fashion.

Biblical Jesus followers claim that the Historical Jesus actually and physically worked at least some of the miracles and cures. They are unsure of the nature miracles, where Jesus stops storms and causes a fig-tree to wither, but they are more sure of the cure of bodily ills. They introduce modern medical ideas regarding recognised forms of hysteria to show that sometimes Jesus may have simply elicited a placebo effect to mentally-challenged people; he persuaded people to cure themselves, they claim, or became convinced they were no longer inhabited by evil spirits.

Then, there were the cured lepers. They point out that 'leprosy' covered a wide range of serious and not so serious skin ailments from Hansen's disease to psoriasis to eczema. They claim that Jesus changed people's attitudes to these unsightly conditions, considered as rendering the sick ritually unclean, but did not cure the medical conditions themselves. Some Biblical Jesus scholars say that this change in onlookers' bias was the 'cure'. Likewise these scholars point to modern-day psychotherapy as 'the casting out of demons', the alleviation of mental illness.

It can be annoying to follow their tracks. The Biblical Jesus scholars are willing to construct an exact chronology of Jesus events from the material in the four gospels, disregarding the place of a particular story in the particular gospel structure. They reconcile obvious discrepancies by ingenuous means. The Birth Narrative in Matthew is combined with the Birth Narrative in Luke, two quite different stories. The Passion stories in the four gospels are combined to produce a running account that could be submitted to modern legal scrutiny in Jesus' favour. There are seven Last Words spoken by Jesus on the cross, despite the fact that no one gospel has seven.

Without going further, I need to say that this Biblical Jesus never existed; the exercise has no purpose in the Christian religion, in literature or in history. The project should be discontinued immediately.

*Hence Literary Israel has led us to the Literary Jesus. The Literary Jesus is presented as the human This-worldly Intermediary who can connect a community with the God of Israel. Literary Jesus corrects one important item in the religion of Judaism. Who is the This-worldly Intermediary? Not king, prophet, Hasmonean priest-king but Jesus of Nazareth. Being a replacement Intermediary means that he has established something new, a new form of Jewish religion. But by the time of John's gospel, after the turn of the second century, there has been a complication. Jesus became not only the This-worldly Intermediary but also the Other-worldly Intermediary, a divine being.*

*This has been the beginning of what we are seeking, the replacement of other Jewish forms of Intermediary by the Literary Jesus. At the very first, this Literary Jesus was known in a Tradition, collections of oral tradition handed on by word of mouth and only gradually being written down. But who would succeed the Literary Jesus?*

Succession, we have seen, is of vital importance. There is no continuation for a religion without succession. Peter was never named in the Sayings Gospel Q, but by the time of the Synoptic gospels and their Literary Jesus he was clearly the successor to Jesus. He was first mentioned in the list of The Twelve by Mark and became the official spokesman for the disciples at the very centre of the gospel. His role was spelled out in more detail in Matthew. But this was all written some thirty odd years after the events.

As already said, in John, the matter is not so clear. There were a number of contenders for the successor of Jesus: certainly Peter, but also Mary Magdalene and the 'Beloved Disciple'. Behind the Gospel of John there were early groups of mystics who did not need a This-worldly Intermediary. They only required a Teacher. But that is another matter.

In short, there is no real evidence in the Story of Literary Jesus (and certainly not in any reconstruction of Historical Jesus) that there had been a formal transfer of authority from Jesus solely to Peter. There were other possible contenders.

We now need to return to our historical research and examine the early events of the time after Jesus. This is the time of the Jesus-movements. From this investigation we hope to extract more information on the succession to Jesus.

## NOTES

Some excellent books on the background of the Historical Jesus are:

Crossan, J. and Reed, J. (2001), *Excavating Jesus: Beneath the Stones, Behind the Texts*, HarperSanFrancisco: New York

Freyne, S. (2004), *Jesus, a Jewish Galilean. A New Reading of the Jesus Story*, T. and T. Clark International (Continuum): London and New York.

Freyne, S. (2000), *Galilee and Gospel. Selected Essays*, J.C.B. Mohr: Tübingen

# 3/
# THE CHURCH STORY – 'PETER'

What resulted after the death of the Historical Jesus was the emergence of the Jesus-movement. But, to complicate things, there were more than one Jesus-movement. Memories of the Historical Jesus were transformed into the first formulations of the Literary Jesus, not haphazardly but with purpose. These formulations included the accounts of Jesus' ministry and death, together with the reports that in some way he continued to be a 'living Jesus' after a resurrection from an Empty Tomb. The coming-to-be Literary Jesus accompanied and even stimulated the rise of a number of disparate groups within Judaism at that time. They would each broadly interpret him within the context of a Jewish Just One or a Jewish Messiah or, later, a Divine Son of God.

We will now go back to the notion of Jewish Messiahship. Jews generally expected that their suffering life, under first the Greeks and then the Romans, had to get better than what it was. Betterment would require some sort of divine intervention, and this sometimes involved the intervention of God's 'Messiah' or Anointed One, a term taken from Literary Israel. As already noted, some Jews evidently expected one or more military type messiahs, others one or more peaceful messiahs. There was also at certain times an expectation of a diarchy, two messiahs in tandem, of whom one would be a military commander and the other a priest. This seems to be the expectation in one of the Dead Sea Scrolls documents. There were doubtless Jews who expected not a particular person or persons but a messianic transformation, a more vague divine intervention of some sort. At a time when there did not seem to be a recognisable This-worldly Intermediary in the offing, the search turned to the future.

In this Jewish context, some Jews interpreted Jesus as God's Messiah, but they did so only after his death. Others continued to see him as the Just One, an exalted Jewish holy man, still others began to see him as divine, a Son of God who knew all things, who had been sent with a mission from Yahweh himself. In all these guises he was an Intermediary. As a result, more than one early Christian group was generated and they each had their leader who was seen in some way as a successor to Jesus.

If we are going to understand Christian leadership, and eventually Papal power, we must first understand these groups, their leaders and their claims to leadership and what became of the groups.

After the death of the Historical Jesus, the Literary Jesus was being constructed. But there was to be yet more construction. How did the first Christians, looking back, interpret the events from the time of the Literary Jesus (who was resurrected) to themselves? This is the Church Story. It is not history. It is an interpretation of how they saw themselves come to be as they were.

We have already noted that the first Church Story, for which we have a substantial text, is the Acts of the Apostles. It was brought up to date by The Ecclesiastical History written by Eusebius of Caesarea written in the fourth century.

### The Successors to Jesus

Jesus died by execution. The process of transforming the Historical Jesus into the Literary Jesus began at once. There were many Literary Jesus-es. There were many Jesus-movement groups. There were many claims to be successors to Jesus.

There was one group headed by James, who was called by Paul, Luke and other early writers 'the Brother of the Lord' and known in his own time as James the Just. It would seem that this group was known as 'The Brothers', as the term is used in Acts 12:17. Peter, having been released from prison, tells his own group before he leaves for 'another place': 'Tell this to James and to the Brothers'. The 'Brothers' therefore seem to be clearly living in a different location within Jerusalem to Peter and the Twelve. In the course of time copyists, not understanding the relevance of the term, changed the original 'Brothers' in the Greek text to 'Believers'.

The written material (outside the Christian canon of writings) on James extends his identification as a Just One, the same title as given to Jesus. We will first examine the evidence in Josephus concerning the death of James. Josephus tells how Festus, the procurator of Judaea, died in office and was succeeded by Albinus. The interregnum provided Ananus, the Sadducean[17] High Priest appointed by Herod Agrippa II, an opportunity to rid himself of James. James was brought before the Sanhedrin and sentenced to death. The sentence was immediately carried out. Ananus was deposed by Agrippa for this unlawful action.

The fact that the texts emphasise that James was the blood brother of Jesus, seem to infer a dynastic succession. In other words, the Brothers of the Lord were led by James the Just, a brother of Jesus, who was considered by his followers to be the successor to Jesus the Just. James had the solid backing of a Vision of Jesus after his death giving him right of succession. The most explicit description of this vision was handed on in the non-canonical *Gospel according to the Hebrews*:

> (Jesus) took bread and gave thanks and broke it, and then gave it to James the Just, saying to him: 'My brother, eat your bread because the Son of Man has risen from those who sleep.' (As quoted in Jerome's *De Viris Illustribus* 2.)

After James' death his successor as leader of The Brothers was Simeon, son of Clopas and hence a cousin of Jesus. Then there was a series of other successors, but always from within the family of Jesus. For a while at least, during the Roman suppression of revolt, some of the community went to Pella in the north, probably around 67 CE. This was looked upon by many Jews in Jerusalem as treachery. It would have undermined the authority of the Brothers of the Lord. Probably most of the group returned later after the destruction of Jerusalem and by then the tradition was established that this destruction had been divine retaliation for the execution of James. The Brothers disintegrated for the same reason as other more mainstream Jewish groups: their Temple had been destroyed.

However, the Synoptic gospels and the Gospel of John are adamant that the family of Jesus, including his brothers, had viewed his public activities with jaundiced eyes. In fact this leads to the denial on the part of the Literary Jesus in the Synoptics that he even wishes to retain such blood relationships. The groups associated with the Synoptics must have severed connections with the Brothers of the Lord. Luke includes James in his Church Story but eventually he is displaced by Paul.

The Synoptic gospels were generated within another Jesus-movement, the Peter group. This group also claimed a Vision for its leader, Peter. It is recorded in a variety of gospel traditions: Jesus appears to Peter and commends the flock to him, after Peter had seen the Empty Tomb. But the Synoptics are clear, particularly Matthew, that even in his lifetime Peter had been given the role of successor and full authority over the future Jesus-movement.

Connected with the Peter group was another group. It was headed by John, who was named by Paul as one of the three 'pillars' of the Jerusalem community. This group relied for its leadership upon a John. Despite the fact that this group seems to have had connections with Gnosticism (about which more will be said), at some point this Jesus-movement merged with the Peter group. There was the need for compromise. John's resurrection account highlights the primary role of the Beloved Disciple, whose identity is hotly contested. Peter and the Beloved Disciple are rival successors. We can only conjecture that the John group was subsumed in the Peter group and the Gospel of John was amended accordingly.

Peter's group must have lost credibility with other Jews in Jerusalem because of his own practice of consorting with Gentiles. James of Zebedee (an early follower of Jesus and not his brother) was executed as a result and Peter was imprisoned. This setback could have given the opportunity for James the Just to take a more dominant role and assert authority: he wanted to continue Jewish ritual observance; he wanted meals to be held separately when non-observant Jesus people came together with observant ones, a move which would have obviated the need for circumcision of the non-observant followers. At that time circumcision without adequate anaesthesia or antiseptics was a dangerous procedure particularly for adults.

The Jesus-movements were causing agitation among the Jews and that was always a problem in volatile Jerusalem. Peter was eventually forced to leave Jerusalem because of the political pressure and it seems he went to Antioch, then a Roman outpost.

From Antioch, Peter could have gone to Rome via Corinth after he heard of the death of Claudius, who had been antipathetic to the Jesus-movement, in 54. Whatever the date, he must at some time have gone to Rome. Certainly all texts that speak of Peter's death maintain that it took place in Rome and he was buried there. No other city is a contender and there certainly would have been contenders if there was any doubt at all about the place of his death and internment.

There were other groups and we can discover them hidden beneath the Church Story in Acts. For example, there were the Hellenists led by Stephen, together with a group led by an unknown leader, Apollos (also mentioned in Paul's letters). These groups were all Jesus-movement factions within a rather disorganised Jewish community of that time. Luke would eventually gloss over the divisions and their complex relationships in the Acts of the Apostles, but he was interested in the Church Story and not in history.

The Hellenists were the most radical. Where they derived their name from we are unsure. Perhaps they belonged to a particular synagogue in Jerusalem that attracted a Greek-speaking or Hellenist clientele (not that speaking Greek in Jerusalem would have been so unusual). Their leader was a Stephen, otherwise unknown. These Hellenists maintained that, because of the advent of Jesus, Judaism had been superseded and the sacrificial system and the other rituals carried out in the Temple should be forthwith discontinued. This was very subversive and disturbing talk and it soon aroused the ire of fellow Jews and, more ominously, the suspicion of the Romans.

No doubt this talk led to more violent physical exchanges. Stephen was executed by the Jews on the grounds of his blasphemy against Moses. The Jewish authorities were probably authorised by their Roman superiors to carry out such an execution and the Romans would have been quite pleased to see a disturber of the peace dispatched.

Stephen's followers fled up the Palestinian coast. They eventually moved to Cyprus and Antioch and there they found that not only Jews but also some Gentiles were interested in their message, and were willing to become part of their new movement. They must have eventually disappeared for some unknown reason.

Very importantly, there were also the Christian Gnostic groups.

## The Gnostics

The term 'Gnostic' has been created by modern scholars to cover a number of groups of dissident Christians in the early centuries. 'Gnostic' derives from the Greek word for 'knowledge', *gnosis*, which featured highly in their teaching. There were already, at the beginning of the Christian period, Gnostics within Judaism. They had various names for themselves although those in whom we are interested saw themselves as the true followers of Jesus. They were Christian Gnostics.

In the eighteenth and nineteenth centuries the first texts written by the ancient Gnostics, rather than transcriptions of texts by their enemies, were discovered. In December 1945 there was a fortuitous find. It took place in Upper Egypt in an area known as Nag Hammadi, where twelve bound codices or books and the loose leaves of another were uncovered having been buried for many centuries. Altogether, 53 separate texts have been identified in the codices, dated to about 350-400 CE. However, the codices are copies of Greek originals (fragments of which had earlier been found) which go back perhaps to the second century CE. They include gospels – *The Gospel of Thomas*, *The Gospel of Philip*, *The Gospel of Truth*. There was also another gospel, *The Gospel of Mary* (Magdalene), found in the nineteenth century and also the *Gospel of Judas* which came to light recently and was published in the 1990s. The Nag Hammadi texts were probably buried by monks from a nearby Christian monastery who feared the wrath of the army sent by the Roman Emperors to stamp out all deviations from mainline Christianity in the fourth century CE.

From this cache of texts we now know much more about Gnosticism. The Gnostic teachings stressed the need for *gnosis* or knowledge. They claimed that salvation was only possible through a secret knowledge, a revelation, which was reserved for the chosen few. Jesus, in their version of events, came on earth to teach the elect how to achieve that knowledge. For them Jesus was a Teacher and a Saviour, whose main role was to teach *gnosis*.

However, their Jesus was not the Literary Jesus of the canonical gospels of Matthew, Mark, Luke or John (in its present form; it may be based on Gnostic documents). Their Jesus was the Eternal Son of God, timeless and perfect, who never became human since the Gnostics considered all flesh and matter to be inferior and evil, who could not die a real death since he did not have a real body, and therefore did not require a physical resurrection. The elect few or the Gnostics, haters of the world and its attractions, were called to this profound self-knowledge (*gnosis*), and that knowledge led them to see and find this living, eternal Jesus within themselves. They realised their own divinity and became like Jesus.[18] The true Gnostic was the one who profoundly understood the divine mysteries and thus found redemption even before death.

From an early period in the Christian era there were Gnostic groups, other Jesus-movement groups. Some would have been perpetuated or even established by ascetic monks, living an austere life in desert regions. However, other groups may well have included the more general populace. They were regarded by many of the Peter group as The Enemy. They would be effectively wiped out by the Roman military in the fourth century CE.

## Paul and his following

And there was another major leader who had his own Jesus-movement group. This was Paul, whom Luke describes in Acts as having had a startling Vision of Jesus on the road to Damascus. In Galatians 1:15-16 Paul introduces his apostleship with his own description of the experience that is nothing like the dramatic tale of being thrown from his horse and hearing Jesus' voice. He related that God was pleased 'to reveal his Son in me'. This would seem to be an interior experience. He subsequently went to Jerusalem and met with Peter and James. Fourteen years later, Paul went again to Jerusalem and described a meeting with the three 'pillars' – James, Cephas or Peter and John. It would seem that, with some apprehension on their part, they commissioned him as a missionary to go to the more Gentile Western Diaspora or Dispersion of the Jewish people, with the Jesus message.

Paul's first missionary efforts had actually been made among the Eastern Diaspora. By the time the Greeks had come into Palestine (332-63 BCE), Jews were already being forced, by economic, social and political circumstances, to spread out from their homeland into other lands. This movement was known as the Diaspora. There were two Jewish Diasporas. The first was the Eastern Diaspora and it referred to the dispersion of the Jews into the area from Trans-Jordan to Babylonia. There was also a more widespread Western Diaspora, encompassing the area of Asia Minor, Greece, Italy (including Rome), the south of France, the Mediterranean islands, Egypt, Cyrene and Carthage in North Africa. The results of Paul's first endeavours in the East are unknown, but it is presumed that his attempts to spread the Jesus message were not remarkably successful. He had then moved to the West, returning to Antioch in the years 48 and 49 CE. He was working amongst an established and active congregation in Antioch that belonged to the Peter group.

As he moved out into his own ministry further to the West, Paul set up a standard approach. First, he would arrange private meetings under the patronage of some eminent Jewish persons in the community. Then, he would introduce a retinue of about forty of his own Jesus-movement followers who had accompanied him as the initial congregation. Finally, once a community was established and leaders were appointed, Paul would move on, with his core following, to a new node.

For these forays, Paul concentrated on the more Hellenised and Roman cities, particularly those connected with a port and containing a substantial Jewish population. Prior to his arrival, many Jews, living in a thriving Greek city, had found the demands of Judaism and the Torah (such as the dietary requirements, circumcision and strict Sabbath observance) tiresome. Paul's message was welcomed by 'God-fearers', as they were called, those Greeks who were attracted to the teaching and morality of Judaism but were allowed to live outside the restrictions of the Torah. They were not expected to be circumcised or to follow the other customary Jewish practices. These God-fearers also found Paul's Jesus message attractive and they became the focus of Paul's mission. He was poaching them from the mainstream Jews.

Paul's own writing demonstrates that he was in contact with a number of other different Jesus-movement groups. They did not all please him. There was first of all, by his reckoning, the 'circumcision faction' mentioned first of all in his letter to the Galatians:

> For until certain people came from James, he (Peter) used to eat with the Gentiles. But after they came, he drew back and kept himself separate for fear of the circumcision faction. (2:12)

These 'circumcision faction' people may well have belonged to a Jesus-movement, but they would have accepted belief in Jesus only as an adjunct to the strict observance of the Torah requirements, including circumcision.

Paul was ambivalent as to whether converted Jews should continue to practise as Jews, but he was absolutely clear that Gentile converts, the God-fearers particularly, should not take up Jewish practices. This was expressed clearly in Galatians.

Listen! I, Paul, am telling you that if you let yourselves be circumcised, Christ will be of no benefit to you. Once again I testify to every man who lets himself be circumcised that he is obliged to obey the entire law. (5: 2-3)

And Paul ends the diatribe in his letter with the fervent hope that whoever is unsettling the Galatians with talk about the need for circumcision, would instead castrate themselves (5:12)!

So Paul, despite his reverence for what had been accomplished through the Law, is proposing a new morality, a new way of life, in his Letters intended for his converts. It is the typical morality of a bourgeois Greek of the time, based on Greek philosophy but with the mixture of a strict sexual asceticism that admired celibacy above other sexual practices.

Paul was arrested by the Romans after being involved in a brawl in the Temple of Jerusalem. He would have normally been summarily executed but he revealed to the examining authorities that he was a Roman citizen. He was put on a boat to Rome to be assessed there.

In Rome he would mix with the most important of all the Jesus-movement groups.

*Once again it must be stressed that succession was of vital importance for the continuation of the mission built on the Literary Jesus. Succession is always vital to a new religious movement. Unless some sort of succession is set up, the movement dies a sudden death. Succession to Jesus is described, in a very biased way, in the Church Story.*

*It is important to note that after Jesus died there were a number of Jesus-movement groups; that is historical fact and it is glossed over in the Church Story. Their formation is caught up with the question of succession. They included the James group, the Peter group, the John group, the Hellenists, the followers of Apollos (about whom we know nothing), the 'circumcision faction', the Paul group, the Gnostics, and there were surely others. The Church Story tries to amalgamate them into one seamless movement established by Jesus.*

*The first version of the Church Story, the Acts of the Apostles, clearly portrays Peter as the successor to Jesus. His ministry is a continuation of that of Jesus. Then there is Paul. Paul is presented by Luke in The Acts as a replica of Jesus. He has a blinding religious experience, he begins a ministry and is arrested. He is brought before the Roman governor and then sent to the Jewish Tetrarch. Then Paul begins his Way as a Roman prisoner. It leads to Rome, regarded as the centre of civilisation. We are led to believe he is executed in Rome. We will cover this in more detail.*

*This is not the time to identify any one successor to Jesus. There were many. But they would be narrowed down in the Church Story.*

*We now turn to Rome. Rome was the site of the most important Jesus-movement group. Rome was also the key to the question of succession to the Literary Jesus.*

# NOTES

On the question of the religious successors of Jesus, see my own article and its bibliography:

Crotty, R (1996), *'James the Just in the History of Early Christianity'*, Australian Biblical Review, 44, pp.42-52

and there is a good collection of articles in

Byrne R. and McNary-Zak, B. eds. (2009), *Resurrecting the Brother of Jesus: the James Ossuary Controversy and the Quest for Religious Relics*, University of South Carolina Press: Chapel Hill

On Paul, his life and teaching, there is a great deal of material. Some interesting books are:

Crossan, J. and Reed, J. (2004), *In Search of Paul*, HarperSanFrancisco: New York

Wills, G. (2006), *What Paul Meant*, Viking: New York

On Gnosticism see:

Robinson, J. (ed.) (third edition 1990), *The Nag Hammadi Library in English*, HarperSanFranciso, New York

Pagels, E. (1979), *The Gnostic Gospels*, Weidenfeld and Nicolson, London

King, K. (2003), *What is Gnosticism?*, Harvard University Press: Cambridge

On the Beloved Disciple see:

Charlesworth, J. (1995), *The Beloved Disciple. Whose Witness Validates the Gospel of John?*, Trinity Press International: Valley Forge, Pennsylvania.

Linforth, K. (2014), *The Beloved Disciple: Jacob the Brother of the Lord*, VIVID Publishing, Fremantle

# 4/
# ROMAN CHRISTIANITY

To understand how the Jesus-movement came to Rome we must begin with the Jews of the time in that great city. They came to Rome first, ahead of the Christians. Then, a Jesus-movement somehow became embedded in this Roman Jewish structure. How it did so is an intriguing but insoluble question. And how the Peter group became involved with the Roman group is another problem.

However, this is the key to what we are looking for in explaining the creation of the Papacy.

As explained earlier, by the Hellenistic period (332-63 BCE), Jews were being forced, by economic, social and political circumstances, to spread out from their homeland into other lands, into the Eastern Diaspora and the Western Diaspora. Jews had therefore been making their way to Rome throughout that Greek period and into the time of the Roman Empire. What would they have found?

By the first century CE, Rome was the largest and most magnificent city of the ancient world with a population approaching a million.[19] Only in the nineteenth century would a Western city again achieve that size of population.

The first immigrant Jewish arrivals in Rome can probably be dated to the mid-second century BCE. The Jews formed a foreign enclave in the city, mainly in Trans Tiberim, the area on the other side of the Tiber, still today known as Trastevere. Next, in the first century BCE numerous Jewish slaves were brought to Rome as a result of Pompey the Great's conquests in the East, and so the Jewish population in Rome increased. It is assumed that, as time went on, still other Palestinian Jews saw new business opportunities in the capital and migrated to Rome as free merchants.

These immigrant Jews were integrated in some ways into the Roman culture and adopted Roman ways. The family, so crucial to Roman culture, became all important to the Roman Jews as well. Although they have left behind hundreds of unmarked grave sites or sites marked only by crude and grammatically inaccurate scratches, there were also some fine tomb inscriptions These inscriptions reveal that over time there was less and less use of Hebrew or Aramaic and more of the Roman languages, Greek and Latin. However, there is enough evidence to show that the Jewish population of Rome basically retained its own Jewish identity in the face of adapting to Roman culture. Still, no doubt the Romans regarded them as foreign and different, particularly because of their unusual religious practices such as circumcision, Sabbath observance and abstinence from pork.

These Jews in Rome did have some advantages. They had been granted privileges for supporting Julius Caesar, including exemption from military service, permission to collect the Temple tax to send it back to Jerusalem and freedom of worship. Their religion was regarded as a lawful one, a *religio licita*. This meant that they could set up their own synagogues without further authorisation.

And so, for the most part, when we refer to Jews in Rome in the first century CE we are referring to a population of about 20,000 that is composed of Greek-speaking, poor non-citizens, often slaves or ex-slaves as well as merchants and lower-class citizens. Most would have been living in overcrowded *insulae*, multi-storey buildings in Trans Tiberim, under most insanitary conditions. The Jewish community was organised around about eleven autonomous synagogues in Rome, each of them independent, with a 'synagogue ruler' as the leader. However, not all Jews attended the synagogue; the family became the more important focus for their religious practice in Rome.

Who would have brought the Jesus-movement to the Roman Jewish synagogues and Trans Tiberim? It was not Peter who came much later, nor was it Paul who had written to the already existing Jesus-movement members in Rome long before he arrived there in person. Paul even acknowledged in his *Letter to the Romans* that the Roman church was 'someone else's foundation' (15:20) and that he had wanted to visit the Christian group in Rome for many years.

We can only speculate that either Jews – whether they were merchant immigrants, prisoners of war or slaves – who had somehow come into contact with the Jesus-movements in Palestine went to Rome or that Roman Jews had gone to Palestine (perhaps for a pilgrimage? perhaps to celebrate one of the festivals?) and came into contact with the new Jesus-movements there. They would have brought some form of the Story of Jesus back to Rome and introduced it into the Roman synagogues. Perhaps Jesus-movement factions thrived in some synagogues; perhaps entire synagogues were taken over by the new movement. The identification of the founder or founders of Roman Christianity will probably be forever shrouded in anonymity.

### *From Jewish Jesus-movement to Roman Christianity*

However, the Roman Jesus-movement seems to have readily admitted non-Jews, whether 'God-fearers' or converts from paganism, who would not have wanted to continue contact with the synagogues. Then, in a dramatic moment, some of the Jewish Jesus-movement people, attached to the synagogues during the reign of Claudius, were expelled for some years in about 49 CE for stirring up trouble in the synagogues. They set up minor Jesus-movement groups in exile. As a result of the exile of Jewish Jesus-movement people, the Jesus-movement still left in Rome would have been composed mainly or entirely of Gentiles. When the Jewish Jesus-movement exiles returned to Rome after the death of Claudius in 54 CE, they would have found that the Roman Jesus-movement they had left behind had become mainly Gentile. The Roman Jesus-movement people had cut their moorings with the synagogues and moved into house-churches or *ekklesiae*. They no longer identified themselves as Jewish.

The Jesus-movement people in Rome, like the Jews before them, struggled to show that they were good citizens and this was all that Rome required. However, as increasing conversions to the Jesus-movement took place, there were problems. Roman members were abandoning the cults of their Roman ancestors and risking the displeasure of the Roman gods and this was directed not only at the Jesus-movement people but more importantly directed against the State.

At some point when the Jesus-movement people had moved out of the synagogues and into house-churches, when they not only admitted Gentiles but their population was largely Gentile, they could easily be identified as a separate group by Nero and his administration. Nero, the successor to Claudius, persecuted them as Jesus-movement people but did not persecute the Jews themselves. In this way, the Jesus-movement became the Christian Church in Rome. It is only at that time that we can start using the term 'Christian'. This was a disadvantage under Nero; it would later become an advantage when the Jews in Jerusalem revolted against the Romans in Jerusalem. In short, Christians were no longer Jews.

How might Paul and Peter have been related to this community?

Paul had seen the opportunity to introduce himself to the members of the Roman Church around 55/56 or 56/57 CE. He sent them, as related above, a *Letter to the Romans* with the aim of addressing disputes among the Jesus-movement people in Rome about the Jewish Law and the relationship between Jewish and Gentile Christians.

Most attempts to describe the structure of the Jesus-movement at this time relies on the list of Paul's greetings in Romans 16:3-16. The letter is not addressed to a single *ekklesia* or church of Rome, but to the different and separate house-churches. There would seem, on the basis of the greetings, to have been up to seven house-churches. This loose structure of Christianity could be compared to the loose organisation of Judaism in Rome, with a number of synagogues, but with no overarching authority.

Only one *ekklesia* is named, one hosted by Aquila and Priscilla, a couple mentioned in the *Letter* and also in the text of Acts. The best explanation for the Romans text is that the *ekklesia* in the house of Aquila and Priscilla is asked to greet each other, and twenty-eight names of those in that *ekklesia* are added. There were also some general greetings. In other words, by the mid-50s CE, the Jesus-movement in Rome only consisted of some dozens of members. The Jesus-movement Gentiles were regarded as equals with the Jews in their community. Paul asked in his *Letter*: what should be the relationship of Roman Jesus-movement people, who did maintain strict observance of the Law, and those members who did not?

He was faced with a rather stark reality: the Jews believed that Yahweh had set up a covenant or treaty with their people, and the Torah provided the framework of their response to this covenant, and the Torah also provided the means of atonement for transgressions. Observance of the Torah would seem to be a significant sign of belonging to God's chosen people.

In contrast, Paul argues in the early part of *Romans* that the gospel message is not limited to Jews, and then later he struggles to explain how this fact is not opposed to the status of Israel as the chosen people: belief in Jesus has itself constituted a chosen people.

The major theme of *Romans* is then enunciated: Jesus has reconciled Jew and Gentile by his death. Paul gave an answer to the burning, central question raised by himself in the *Letter to the Romans*: is the Jesus-movement still Jewish? He answered by defining the True Israel: negatively, it is not based on Jewish ancestry, nor on circumcision, nor on dietary observance nor the observance of holy days; positively, the True Israel is a community that participates in the death and resurrection of Jesus and becomes a living community united by the Spirit, and this community is achieved by baptism and the celebration of the Eucharist. These two rituals, Baptism and Eucharist were, according to Paul, the essentials of Christian liturgical practice and the Death and Resurrection of Jesus were the keystone beliefs.

Paul came to Rome. Paul would have felt at home with the Roman Jesus-movement with its breakaway from formal Judaism. He was later depicted as another Jesus who came to them and was then executed like his Master.

But the Church Story is true to Peter too. The Roman Jesus-movement was founded on the Literary Jesus, as portrayed in the Synoptics, who had appointed Peter. They portray Peter as the successor to Jesus, chosen by Jesus himself during his lifetime. In the time of Nero's persecution of 64 CE, Peter seems to have gone to Rome, probably to support the Jesus-movement there. The second motive might have been to resolve a crisis in the Roman community after the departure or death of Paul. The crisis may have been the resurgence of conflict between the Torah-observant and the non-observant in the Jesus-movement. Luke leaves the question of leadership open – both Peter and Paul are successors to Jesus. Towards the end of the second century, the Christian writer and bishop of Lyons in France, Irenaeus, still accepted that the Roman Church was founded by both Peter and Paul.

This is not history. It is the Church Story narrated by Luke.

During the later 60s CE all the Jews of Rome must have lived in great uncertainty and the Jesus-movement members to a lesser extent. In 66 CE the Jews in Palestine had revolted against Rome. The Roman Jews must have been regarded with suspicion by the Roman authorities. Nero's death in 68 CE brought chaos to the capital with three pretenders to the throne ruling and being disposed of in the one year of 69 CE. Order only came with the accession of the general Vespasian. Jerusalem had fallen to his son, Titus, and the Roman army and the spoils of war, including Jewish prisoners, were brought back to Rome in 71 CE.

By the end of the first century Jews and Christians had gone their separate ways in Rome. Between that time and the middle of the third century, the Jesus-movement in Rome consolidated. It was a well-constructed society. Cornelius, the Bishop of Rome from 251 to 253 CE incidentally lists in a letter the administrative members of the Roman church: 46 elders or presbyters, 7 deacons, 7 sub-deacons, 42 acolytes, 52 exorcists and over 1500 widows and indigents. These numbers reflect a total Christian population of something in the tens of thousands; it also reflects a city-wide organisation. The Roman Jesus-movement had become the Christian Church in the West. And it certainly was not Jewish.

*The Jesus-movement in Rome began in the Jewish synagogues in Trans Tiberim. Its founder or founders are unknown. At some stage either early or later this Roman Jesus-movement had come into contact with the Peter group. Perhaps the beginning of the Jesus-movement in Rome was an offshoot of the Peter group. They constructed their Literary Jesus on the basis of the traditions of the Peter group. The three Synoptic gospels are all linked to Rome and the Jesus-movement there.*

*Due to the forced exile of Jewish movement people by the emperor Claudius, Gentile and non-observant Jesus-movement people moved away from the synagogues and founded typically Roman house-churches. This was the beginning of 'Christianity', something quite separate from the Jesus-movements elsewhere.*

*Paul came to Rome. We know nothing else. Later, Peter came and was quickly executed, possibly for stirring up trouble. In the Church Story as related by Luke they are both presented as Successors to Jesus. Eventually, Peter will become the Successor and Paul will be relegated to the role of an esteemed apostle.*

*It is vital for us to understand more of this Roman Jesus-movement. In order to do so, we will look at two archaeological sites in Rome.*

*They both shed historical light on the question we are pursuing: what was the origin of the Church in Rome and the Roman papacy? However, note that we once again move out of the Church Story into history.*

## Clement and his house-church

One of the more revealing texts from the final years of the first century CE is 1 *Clement*, a letter written from Rome to the Christian community in Corinth. It would have been written in the mid-90s and seems to reflect the dire times of the Emperor Domitian's reign.

By the late second century, Christian writers had identified its author as 'Clement' and Irenaeus added that this Clement had been the 'bishop of Rome'. He was also mentioned by the Christian writer Hermas (*Vision 2.4.3*) as one who had the responsibility for addressing other churches, outside Rome, on behalf of Roman Christians, a sort of foreign minister.

His role as Christian foreign minister would explain why he would have written a letter to the Christians in Corinth. Clement was probably a freedman (since his name, Clemens, is Latin, yet he writes in Greek) who had taken his ex-master's cognomen, a common practice. He would therefore have been connected with a more exalted Clemens and possibly it was Titus Flavius Clemens, married to his own cousin, Flavia Domitilla, who was well known. This Clemens was also a cousin to the emperors Titus and Domitian. He held the important position of consul in the administration of Domitian, but he was charged with 'atheism' and executed. His wife was exiled.

Clement the freedman does not write to the Corinthians as one with any authority over its church. He acts as a counsellor, trying to assist a related church group in their difficulty. From the tenor of the letter the problem referred to householders who had charge of house-churches and had therefore taken on the title of *episkopos* or bishop, fighting for recognition over those who had previously been appointed *presbyteroi* or elders.

Authority structures in the various Christian communities in the first century had taken a number of forms. Only in the last quarter of that century had any sort of uniform structure begun to emerge. The death of the great leaders – James the Just, Peter, John and Paul – in the 60s had left a vacuum. The vacuum is important. If these people had been commissioned as Intermediaries by Jesus, who replaced them?

By the 80s the bishop/elder model was widespread. The first letter of Clement acknowledges *episkopoi* or bishops, *presbyteroi* or elders and *diakonoi* or deacons. He presumes that the elders and bishops have a liturgical role to play; the *diakonoi* are more involved with administration. The *episkopoi* and *presbyteroi* also have certain rights because of their succession and here Clement follows the Peter group theology: The Twelve had made the first appointment of bishops and elders; these then handed on the offices to successors. This is important.

Clement assumed that the deposed presbyters in Corinth were in the right and that 'jealousy and envy' were the motives for the usurpation of their authority. His siding with the established authority certainly seems to be based on his understanding of a house-church as being an extended family. Each leader of a house-church is compared to a *paterfamilias* or family-father, who therefore had authority over the members and should be respected. It was a very Roman solution. This reinforcement of traditional authority by Clement is the first clear statement advocating a self-perpetuating church leadership for Christianity.

Clement therefore identified the expelled presbyters as the successors of the Twelve in Corinth. The house-churches with this authority supported by the doctrine of succession must have been the elementary building blocks of Christianity in Rome at the end of the first century. Each house-church, like the Jewish synagogue system that had preceded them, would have been autonomous. While it might have been possible for a Clement to speak on behalf of Roman Christianity to an outside world, he would have been speaking on behalf of a network of individual cells that met separately in the homes of patron-leaders. There is no evidence of any central authority in Rome at that time.

This conjectural reconstruction from *1 Clement* can be reinforced by some archaeological evidence. The archaeological work under the still-standing church of San Clemente is most interesting. The church stands in an area near the Colosseum, once owned by the Flavians.

Nero, after the great fire of 64 CE, had hoped to use the same land to extend his urban villa, the sumptuous *Domus Aurea*, the Golden House. The fire had destroyed most of the public buildings in the area and Nero took advantage of the opportunity. He demolished everything to make way for his palace. The common people of Rome, for the most part living in crowded and inhumane conditions, did not appreciate the grandiose scheme he had in mind.

After Nero, the Flavians inherited this land. When Vespasian came to power he wanted to appease the aggrieved people by discontinuing the building of the Golden House and giving the area over to public works. He drained a central lake and began construction of the Flavian Amphitheatre (later known as the Colosseum) as a public arena for games and gladiator battles. It was a popular decision. While the circuses attracted all classes of Roman inhabitants, they were particularly an outlet for the destitute poor who could forget their unhappy lot while involved in the blood-letting games. The building of the Colosseum was continued under Titus and Domitian. Buildings surrounded the Colosseum to house, supply and train the gladiators, to administer the amphitheatre and see to its upkeep. By the end of the first century CE the area also contained the Baths of Titus, the Baths of Trajan (which covered over part of the unfinished Golden House) and the official Roman Mint.

Jerome, the great biblical scholar, had written, sometime around 392 CE, that in this very area 'a church in Rome preserves the memory (*memoria*) of Saint Clement to this day'. Up until the nineteenth century it was believed that the present day church of San Clemente was the one to which Jerome referred.

However, in 1857 Joseph Mullooly, a Dominican priest, began an amateur archaeological dig underneath the present-day church (which he dated to the twelfth century CE) and within a year discovered the north aisle of a fourth century basilica and, digging further beneath this earlier basilica, he found a room which was later to be identified as the anteroom to a Temple of Mithras. Later, in 1860, he discovered directly beneath the fourth century basilica, two levels down, another building from the first century. Between this newly discovered building and the Mithras temple there was a laneway. All of these lower buildings had been filled in with debris to serve as a solid foundation for the fourth century church.

Later excavations have since extended Mullooly's dig. As a result of nearly a century and a half of patient archaeological investigation we are today able to recreate the stages of architectural growth on the site. At the very lowest level there is a stratum of fire-ravaged debris, which is about eleven metres below the present ground level. This can be dated to the fire of 64 CE in Nero's reign; it was the only extensive fire known in that area. The gutted buildings and wreckage were filled in by the Flavians and used as foundations for new public buildings.

The building under San Clemente at the lowest level consisted of a rectangular structure built from large tufa bricks. It consists of a large open courtyard with perimeter rooms of which some fifteen have been so far excavated. It would seem therefore that it can be dated to the latter third of the first century. Its purpose? Some think it could be the Roman Mint, which has not been discovered elsewhere so far; others think that it was linked to the Colosseum in some way. However, because of its curious architecture (the walls are very thick and there are no external windows) archaeologists tend to conclude that it was a Warehouse (a *horreum*).

Sometime after this tufa building was completed, another red brick building was constructed next to it. We know that this building was built later because it used the western wall of the tufa building for support by means of a bridge of bricks over a laneway. The brick stamps on this second building date it to the 90s. It consisted of two floors. On the ground floor there was a large room surrounded on all sides by corridors and smaller rooms around its perimeter. A second floor covered the first, but we are unsure of its layout. The ground floor building seems clearly to have been meant for living quarters. But who would have lived there? Gladiators? Members of the Flavian family? There is no evidence on which to draw a firm conclusion. However, we do know that the ground floor of this brick building was, either in the second or third century CE, converted for use as a Temple of Mithras.[20]

In the fourth century CE the Warehouse was filled with rubble and used as the foundation for a church in honour of St Clement, identified as a Bishop of Rome. This was the church to which Jerome referred. The Temple of Mithras must have continued to function. However, we know that, after Constantine and certainly by the time of Theodosius' edict in 395 CE, foreign cults such as Mithraism were outlawed. At some point in the fourth century its cult would have been stopped. The whole building must have then been acquired by the church authorities, who possessed the adjoining basilica, and the former Temple area was used to serve as an apse for the basilica in the early fifth century.

This church dedicated to St Clement lasted some eight centuries until it began to decay. In the twelfth century the decision was made to demolish it and fill the space between its walls with rubble to the top of the pillars. A new basilica, on a somewhat smaller scale, was then erected on top of this platform.

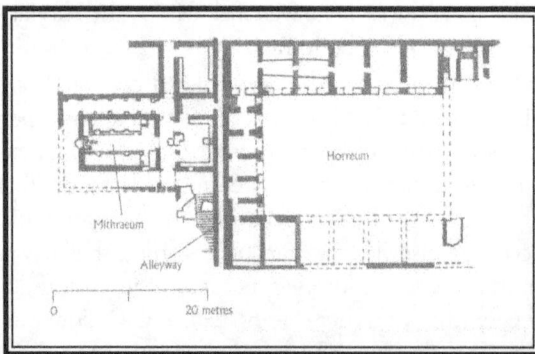

Figure 5
Plan of the area under San Clemente with Mithraeum and Horreum side by side.

Jerome's reference to a 'church of St Clement' would have meant the fourth century building minus its apse. He stated that it was a *memoria* or a *memorial* of St Clement. Sometimes the term *memoria* refers to the place where a saint was buried, but it is well documented that the human remains of Clement had been elsewhere and they were only brought to the church in the ninth century. The original basilica was therefore not over his tomb. What was it about the church that could have been a *memorial*?

Since the first basilica had been built over the tufa walled building, then somehow this building must have been connected with 'Clement' and the only Clement of any fame in the period before Jerome was the author of *1 Clement*, which we examined above. Without being able to prove it with any certainty, there is evidence that the tufa building was this Clement's house-church. It would have become, in the third century, a church administrative centre as was the common practice. But, how had it functioned as a house-church earlier, so close to the Colosseum and next to a Temple of Mithras?

What follows is an historical reconstruction based on what we have found from the text of *1 Clement* and the archaeological reports. The consul, Titus Flavius Clemens, came into possession of the area where these particular buildings were situated, after the death of Nero. The residential building (not yet a Temple of Mithras) might have been used by him as a residence for his family, next to a warehouse, which could have served his business interests. There is evidence that he and his wife, Flavia Domitilla, either became Jesus-movement people or sympathised with them. He was executed on Domitian's orders because of this religious aberration, called 'atheism' (Suetonius commented that his execution was 'on the most flimsy evidence'), while Flavia Domitilla was exiled.

The couple might have allowed Christians to meet in part of the tufa building, the Warehouse, perhaps in a room or perhaps in the central courtyard. It became a house-church. These Christians would have enjoyed the protection of one of the more powerful couples on the Roman scene. The leader of the house-church was not the consul, but one of his freedmen, Clement.

The house-church was later known as *Titulus Clementis*. These early house churches were known by the name (*titulus*) of its founder and by the fourth century we know of twenty-five of them in Rome.

We are at this point close to the basic building-blocks of Roman Christianity. The Christians, forced by circumstances, and especially the decree of Claudius, to leave the synagogues, established house-churches as substitutes. Each house-church was autonomous and each looked back to a patron-owner. Because of the Roman concept of family, authority was vested in the male patron, and his authority was said to have derived from The Twelve and Peter. There is no evidence of a centralised church in Rome or of an overall leader. Clement (incorrectly named in later lists as the third Pope), was an influential local house-church leader whose fame allowed him to write to another house-church in Corinth and offer counsel.

How and when the house-churches of Rome had accepted the Peter group's version of the Literary Jesus we may never know. Perhaps the initial founders had been in contact with the Peter Jesus-movement in the East. Perhaps later arrivals brought the Peter version. Soon after Peter had come to Rome (and was presumably welcomed as was, in a much later time, Ayatollah Khomeini to Teheran), and executed, some form of the Gospel of Mark was written enshrining the Literary Jesus of the Peter tradition for the Roman Church. This was elaborated on but affirmed by the Gospel of Matthew. But this acclamation was somewhat distorted by the fact that Luke's Acts of the Apostles highlighted the role of Paul. Peter and Paul were made joint-Successors.

The second archaeological site is under the present-day St Peter's.

## The site under St Peter's

An even more striking excavation took place under St Peter's, beginning in 1939 with digging under the nave and continuing during World War II. A necropolis or cemetery was uncovered that had been expanding from the mid-second CE to the early fourth century CE on a slope of the Vatican hill. It contained splendid mausolea, small houses with artistically worked tombs within, altars and fine sculptures, belonging to upper class Romans. These were intersected by pathways.

Constantine had expropriated the necropolis in the fourth century CE, cutting back the upper sections of some of the mausolea to the north and filling in and burying those to the south with rubble. Families must have been given the opportunity to remove the remains of their forebears (no human remains were found), but they could not remove the furnishings – altars, murals, sculptures. Over the expanse he constructed a huge platform as the foundation of the first basilica of St Peter. The platform would have taken enormous labour and skill and Constantine broke all Roman law in interfering with the mausolea and their dead occupants.

Why such expenditure and effort to construct this basilica on the slope of a hill? The excavations showed that the present high altar is positioned above a rather ordinary monument once built up against a wall in the cemetery. Certainly the belief over the ages has been that the church was built over the tomb of Peter. The monument could be the one referred to by a Christian elder, Gaius, at the end of the second century CE as a *tropaion* or shrine, not necessarily a tomb, recalling the presence of Peter in Rome. He was arguing about the authority for Christian teaching and upholding that of Rome over other churches because Peter and Paul were the founders of the church there.

But I can point out the *tropaia* of the apostles; for if you go to the Vatican or the Ostian way, you will find the *tropaia* of those who founded this church.

Leaving aside the interpretation of the excavations, the important point is that Constantine had inherited a tradition that Peter was buried in or under the shrine on the Vatican hill and that this *memorial* to Peter was of vital importance to him.

*Figure 6*
*The area with the tropaion under*
*the high altar in St Peter's*

What preceded this decision of Constantine was an earlier narrowing of the succession tradition in the Church Story. It claimed that Jesus had chosen Peter as his successor or vicar – not James, not Stephen, not John, certainly not Mary Magdalene. In fact, the texts that identify Peter and

Paul as joint successors ceased. It was now claimed that Peter had gone to Rome as its supreme leader, the This-worldly Intermediary. It was claimed that the patrons of the house-churches of Rome derived their authority from Peter, the designated leader of the Twelve. The gospels of Mark and Luke (who had, nevertheless, tried to put Paul on an equal footing with Peter in the Acts) allude to this. Matthew expands on it and makes it much clearer. John is ambivalent.

We know that only in the mid-second century CE did a single ruler in Rome, a monarchic *episkopos*, preside over the other Roman leaders in their respective house-churches, no doubt due to social pressure, the need for stability and organisation. This person became regarded as the direct successor of Peter, but there would have been a gap of some hundred years between Peter and the first designated leader. A later attempt was made to bridge the gap by a succession list (more will be said about such a list in the next chapter). Around this time the shrine or *tropaion* would have been erected in the cemetery in Peter's memory. Perhaps it did not mark a tomb or even the place of martyrdom, but was simply a memorial erected in an existing necropolis to a revered religious figure.

In short, the Roman Jesus-movement, more quickly than elsewhere, had broken its links with Judaism. It became a Christian church. At first it was a loose confederation of house-churches with patrons and local leaders. Then, gradually the authority to rule and speak for the whole of Rome was vested in a single leader and this leader was seen as the successor to Peter. The Peter group had always maintained that Jesus had appointed Peter as the original leader of the Jesus movement; now, Roman Christians saw the Bishop of Rome as the successor to Peter. Constantine made much of this link and the first Saint Peter's Basilica sums up his theological thinking. The archaeological findings support all of this.

*Figure 7*
*St Peter's Basilica*

Constantine ruled Rome as Emperor. He wanted the fact that the successor of Jesus had lived and died in Rome to be commemorated. Instinctively, Constantine knew that this was important for himself. It would extend his own glory. Rome was the centre of Emperor and Empire, Pope ('Peter') and Church.

## Roman Christianity returns to the East

At first there would have been the distinction between Roman Christianity and the more Jewish forms of the Jesus-movement still operating in the East. There would have been less difference between Roman Christianity and the churches set up by Paul in the Western Diaspora. The differences were not to last. The Roman Church began to turn back to the East, from where it had, centuries before, derived its version of the new Jesus-movement.

From around 75-85 CE the Jesus-movement in Rome had severed any direct connection with the Palestinian Jesus-movements. It had its own version of the Literary Jesus in the gospels of Mark, Matthew and Luke. This distinctive form of Roman Christianity was based on house-churches and with elders who honored Peter, the man who had visited them and died among them.

Then, from the late first century or early second century CE, Roman Christianity travelled in the opposite direction to the eastern regions of the Empire, first borne by Roman pilgrims visiting the key sacred places mentioned in the Synoptic gospels and later by Christians connected with the Roman administration (merchants, political appointees, military). There, Roman Christianity met some of the still existing Palestinian forms of the Jesus-movement.

For example there was a Jesus-movement community in Capernaum, a modest village on the Sea of Galilee where the Gospel of Mark maintained that Jesus established his Galilean mission in Peter's house. The village was small, covering some twenty-five acres and would have supported a population of about one thousand. Its buildings were made up of a series of rooms (usually formed by solid ceiling beams supporting a thick bed of reeds and then covered with mud) clustered around a common courtyard.

Dating back to the fifth century CE, archaeologists have found that an octagonal church was venerated, containing within its walls the presumed house of Peter. Around that time the Jews had built a synagogue close by. The remains of the so-called house of Peter have been excavated and they reveal a curious series of adaptations. The top stratum is the fifth century church. But, prior to that, there was a fourth century house-church and beneath this was a courtyard home, a focal point of interest since its walls had been covered over many years with graffiti by pilgrims.

How can these excavations be interpreted? In Capernaum the fourth or fifth century Byzantine church had been built on top of the courtyard home which had been remodelled in the late first century and plastered. In the latter part of the second century this plastered wall had been daubed with graffiti, some undoubtedly written by Christians. Then in the fifth century the room had been enlarged and its ceiling formed into an arch. This is an early shrine doubtless honouring the memory of Peter, whose house was said to be in Capernaum in the Synoptic gospels. Whether this was really over the house of Peter is immaterial; Roman Christians coming to the village thought it was.

But the uncovered building need not necessarily have ever been a community church for local Jesus-movement people; they would have used the nearby synagogue. They would not have had the version of the Literary Jesus (including the succession of Peter) as in the Gospel of Mark. The house shrine honouring Peter would have been a way-chapel catering for wealthy Roman pilgrims from the Empire who subscribed to Roman Christianity. It would have become a flourishing Roman Christian centre after the time of Constantine.

The same is true of other sites such as Nazareth. In the second century pilgrims arrived from various parts of the Empire to see the places mentioned in the canonical gospel traditions, now appropriated by the Roman Church. By that stage the physical landscape had already changed because of the widespread devastation wrought by the upheavals of the two Jewish revolts against Rome. Many landmarks would have been destroyed. The local Jesus-movements were not particularly interested in these historical details.

Nazareth was a rural hamlet in the first century CE. Until the twentieth century it had a Crusader church that was demolished to build a huge modern Basilica in the 1960s. The township in the early first century CE would have accommodated about two to four hundred people. However, in the later imperial period, Nazareth seems to have attracted attention from the pilgrim trade as the hometown of Jesus.

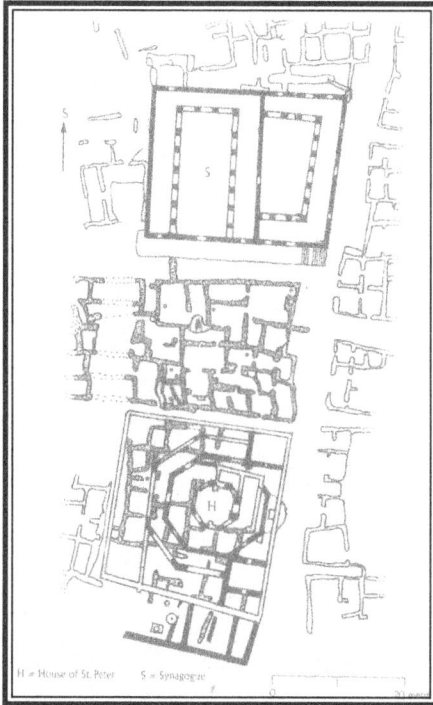

*Figure 8*
*Excavations at Capernaum*
*showing the Synagogue (S)*
*and House of Peter (H)*

The first mention of a Christian shrine in Nazareth comes from Egeria, a pilgrim to the Holy Land in around 383 CE. She sent a long letter back to a group of women, perhaps nuns. This has been retained in only a partial copy, later called the *Travels of Egeria*. She mentions a garden 'in which the Lord used after his return from Egypt', a 'big and very splendid cave' and an altar placed there. The cave and altar probably refer to the larger of the caves in the grotto beneath the present building.

The Crusader church was found to have been built on top of an earlier Greek church. The Greek church had been frequently adorned and there were new floors in mosaic built on top of each other. Beneath this church, there lay three caves with plastered walls, a *mikveh* or Jewish ritual bath and a third century synagogue. It would seem that the caves, whose interiors had been plastered, had been venerated by Christian pilgrims, doubtless as the site of the Annunciation by Gabriel to Mary. However, once again, there is no evidence that we are dealing with a local Jesus-movement church. This would certainly have been a way-chapel, intended for Roman pilgrims, particularly from the Constantinian period.

In other words, there were local Jesus-movement people in places like Capernaum and Nazareth who presumably met and acted ritually like Jews and made use of the local synagogue. They would not have been distinguishable from other Jews of the time. However, they seemed to be catering for a growing number of Roman Christian visitors.

In 326, Constantine's mother Helena followed in the steps of early pilgrims to the East. These pilgrims had been satisfied with local traditions and doubtlessly fabricated sites. She bestowed the imperial seal of approval on certain sites and thenceforward their authenticity would not be questioned until more recent times. And so she identified Golgotha, where Jesus was crucified, and his Empty Tomb nearby. Constantine paid for a large complex to include both sites. He also paid for a basilica to be built over the supposed site of Jesus' birth in Bethlehem. In Jerusalem, yet another site acknowledged the place from which Jesus ascended into Heaven. These were not for the use of locals, but for Roman pilgrims and other visitors.

Certainly by the time of Constantine any juxtaposition between Roman Christianity and the Palestinian Jesus-movements came to an end. Roman Christianity dominated and any remaining Palestinian forms of the Jesus-movement which might have survived atrophied. Roman Christianity, for all practical purposes, was all that remained.

Constantine had recognised the great moments of the Literary Jesus: his birth, his death, his resurrection from the tomb and his ascension into Heaven. But importantly, in Rome, he also commemorated the tomb of Peter with the building of the first Saint Peter's. Peter and Jesus were linked inextricably in his mind.

*Some form of the Jesus-movement had moved from its Palestinian cradle to Rome and it had come back. Within these parameters its character had changed. In Palestine the Jesus-movements, even the original Peter group, would have remained within the confines of Judaism or at least on its perimeter. These Jesus-movements doubtless generated their own literature and society structures.*

*On being transported to Rome, due to historical and social influence (for example, being separated from mainstream Judaism, adapting the Roman culture of the family), the Peter group underwent significant change. This change was written back into its origins and transcribed into the Synoptic gospels. This became the religion of the Roman house-churches, quite separate from the synagogues in Rome, ruled at first by elders and in the mid-second century by a bishop with control over the whole of Rome.*

This new form of Roman Christianity, due to the historical vicissitudes of the Roman period, was taken back into colonial Palestine. There it caused the drastic diminution of any remaining forms of the Jesus-movement. The transformation was completed in the Constantinian period and by the intervention of Constantine himself.

The period of Constantine saw the triumph of Roman Christianity. He simply gave it official recognition and ensured that it became bureaucratic, so it could be part of the State. Rome became Christian and at the same time Christianity became a Roman thing.

Constantine emphasized the Peter element because it suited his plans for a great Rome.

Thus we have advanced from the Literary Jesus as the This-Worldly Intermediary to Peter as his successor to the bishops of Rome as the successors of Peter.

# NOTES

The general theme of this chapter (together with more detail on the two archaeological sites) can be found in my small book:

Crotty, R. (2001), *Roman Christianity: the Distancing of Jew and Christian*, CJCR Press: Cambridge

There are many relevant studies in the following:

Jeffers, J. (1991), *Conflict at Rome. Social Order and Hierarchy in Early Christianity*, Fortress Press: Minneapolis

Donfried, K. and Richardson, P. eds. (1998), *Judaism and Christianity in First-Century Rome*, William B Eerdmans: Grand Rapids

On the return of Roman Christianity to the East see my article,

Crotty R. (2003), 'The Jerusalem Cenaculum as an Early Christian Church Site', *Australian Religion Studies Review*, 16 (1), pp. 24-36

# 5/
# THE ROMAN PAPACY

*We only now, after so much discussion, have sufficient information to look objectively at the 265 or so Popes who succeeded Peter according to the Church Story. When we now speak of 'Christians' we are talking about the Roman Christians and those who divided from them down the ages. We are not talking of the Palestinian Jesus-movements or the Gnostic Christians. This Roman group has been enabled, according to the Church Story, to make contact with the focus on Ultimacy, The Father, through the successor of Peter, the reigning Bishop of Rome. The This-worldly Intermediary is 'Peter'- the original Peter with his successors, the Bishops of Rome.*

*This is Story and not history. It is nonetheless of extreme importance. In fact, history cannot of itself lead to a full understanding of the succession of the Bishops of Rome, the Papacy.*

*In order to understand the birth of the Papacy, we need to know in more detail what happened with regard to the office in the first four or more centuries. That has been the purpose of these preceding chapters.*

*We will see in what follows that the Papacy, the This-worldly Intermediary for the Church's religious followers, changes and is re-fashioned over and over again. Finally, we want to know: what is the shape of the Papacy today? Does it still fulfill its original function? Can it change shape? Is it a capable This-worldly Intermediary?*

*In each of the following sections the list of Popes proper to the discussion will be listed. Not all of them will be discussed or even mentioned further. This book is not simply a catalogue of Popes; it is a discussion on the Papacy.*

✝ Peter (and Paul according to some lists)

✝ Linus

✝ Anacletus (or Cletus)

✝ Clement I

✝ Evaristus

✝ Alexander I

✝ Sixtus I (or Xystus I)

✝ Telesphorus

✝ Hyginus

✝ Pius I

✝ Anicetus (155-166)

✝ Soter (166-175)

✝ Eleutherius (175-189)

In the Church Story, from the evidence we have in *The Acts* and other early writings, there is no universal agreement that Peter was the first Bishop of Rome; in fact, the earliest lists give Peter and Paul as co-founders and co-bishops. Neither is there agreement on the next successor in line.

Turning once more to the bishop of Lyons, Irenaeus, in 180 CE he set out to prove that the teaching of the various Christian churches derived from the Twelve Apostles. He claims that he could trace back any line of bishops from the bishop installed at that time to The Twelve, but he would do so only in the case of Rome. Why does he choose only Rome? He explains:

> For it is a matter of necessity that every Church should agree with this Church (i.e. The Church of Rome), on account of its pre-eminent

authority – that is, the faithful everywhere – inasmuch as the Apostolic Tradition has been preserved continuously by those who are everywhere. (*Adversus Haereses, III, 3*)

He then composed his list, relying on an earlier one from the bishop Anicetus, to show that the Pope of his own time, Eleutherius, could trace his lineage to Peter and Paul:

The blessed apostles (i.e. *both Peter and Paul*), then, having founded and built up the Church, committed into the hands of Linus the office of the episcopate.

His list thereafter includes: Linus, Anacletus, Clement, Evaristus, Alexander, Sixtus, Telesphorus, Hyginus, Pius, Anicetus, Soter and Eleutherius (who was still ruling in Irenaeus' time).

The successors to Peter and Paul in Rome according to Irenaeus are therefore twelve bishops. He makes it clear that Peter and Paul were followed by Linus as bishop of Rome. And there is further confirmation of this. Eusebius (263-339), the earliest Church historian of note, claimed that Linus was 'the first to receive the episcopate of the church at Rome, after the martyrdom of Paul and Peter'. Later, Jerome (347-420), the great Biblical scholar and friend of Popes, wrote that Linus was 'the first after Peter to be in charge of the Roman Church'. There is by this point in time no further mention of Paul. The *Liber Pontificalis* [21], or Book of the Popes, claims that Peter, in order to lighten his burden of rule, ordained two bishops, Linus and Cletus, but he entrusted the Church to Clement. The *Apostolic Constitutions* [22] however, has Linus as first Bishop of Rome after Peter and succeeded by Clement.

It is clear that there has been serious confusion among the writers about the succession. We have already noted that neither Peter nor Paul could have had anything to do with the foundation of the Church in Rome. That was the work of others. In fact, there is no evidence for an overall bishop-leader in Rome until the mid-second century, long after their deaths. These lists are fictive; they belong to the Church Story not to history.

Exactly when in the second century this list of Bishops of Rome would have been composed is uncertain. The process must have been finalised by the time Polycarp, a second century bishop of Smyrna, visited Rome around 155 CE because we read that he met with the bishop Anicetus, who seems to have been in control of the whole of Rome, and they debated the vexed question of how to decide the date of Easter for the entire Church. Anicetus seems to have had the sole power to make such a decision.

It would seem therefore that the list of Popes as found in Irenaeus dates back no further than Anicetus. Twelve bishops were named and that raises doubts (Twelve Tribes of Israel, The Twelve Apostles!). Of the twelve, Peter and Paul were never bishops. Others may have been eminent elders in Rome, such as Clement, but not monarchic bishops. The sixth being Sixtus is particularly suspicious; could there have been an embarrassing gap and the lack of a name? It seems clear that we do not have an historical list. The fact therefore remains, the first time that we hear of one Bishop of Rome is with Anicetus. The important message in the list of twelve is that eleven were believed to be, in the Story of the Church, the successors of Peter who was named first.

Our first list of Popes needs to be taken warily.

*We will now deal with what we know about the Papacy in a time when Popes were certainly elected as Bishops of Rome up to the fifth century. During these early centuries, the election of a Bishop of Rome presumably followed the practice known elsewhere. Clergy and lay people met after the death of a Pope and elected, sometimes by simple proclamation, a new Bishop of Rome. This was sufficient for a fledgling group.*

✝ Victor (189-199)

✝ Zephyrinus (199-217)

✝ Callistus I (217-22)

✝ Urban I (222-30)

✝ Pontain (230-35)

✝ Anterus (235-36)

✝ Fabian (236-50)

✝ Cornelius (251-53)

✝ Lucius I (253-54)

✝ Stephen I (254-257)

✝ Sixtus II (257-258)

✝ Dionysius (260-268)

✝ Felix I (269-274)

✝ Eutychian (275-283)

✟ Caius (283-296). Also called Gaius

✟ Marcellinus (296-304)

✟ Marcellus I (308-309)

✟ Eusebius (309 or 310)

✟ Miltiades (311-14)

✟ Sylvester I (314-35)

✟ Marcus (336)

✟ Julius I (337-52)

✟ Liberius (352-66)

✟ Damasus I (366-83)

✟ Siricius (384-99)

✟ Anastasius I (399-401)

✟ Innocent I (401-17)

✟ Zosimus (417-18)

✟ Boniface I (418-22)

✟ Celestine I (422-32)

✟ Sixtus III (432-40)

✟ Leo I (the Great) (440-61)

✟ Hilarius (461-68)

✟ Simplicius (468-83)

## *The Bishops of Rome and the early spread of Roman Christianity*

It was not until the end of the second century that a Latin name occurs in the lists of bishops of Rome, Victor (189-199). The Church by then had moved well away from its early immigrant Jewish roots in the Roman capital. It continued to expand in the West, but it was now mainly a distinctly Roman thing. The growth had not been remarkable, about 4% percent per year, about the same as the Mormon Church's expansion in modern times. Then, during the reign of Constantine in the fourth century, the Church found the despotic leader who would change everything and enforce growth.

Prior to Constantine there had been in fact long periods of peace, stability and prosperity in the entire Roman Empire. This was an ideal climate for the spread of new ideas: philosophical, technological and religious. The interaction brought about by sailors and merchants plying their trade around the Mediterranean, bringing not only new food and artefacts but much more importantly new ideas, and the advantage of travelling over excellent Roman roads, together with the easy distribution of correspondence and books written in both Greek and Latin, allowed Christian ideas to be disseminated widely.

A new religion like Mithraism, in order to make a new foundation, had to construct sanctuaries according to a very specific design and maintain complex machinery for its intricate practice of animal sacrifice. On the other hand, Christianity in the main only needed its teaching, the inculcation of a moral commitment and the maintenance of a strong belief in an afterlife. These mental attributes were transportable, easily maintained and adaptable. They also found ready acceptance at that time. To a lesser extent it also relied on books.

Christians were acknowledged by this time as a unique religious group, with no connection to Judaism. They had long rejected Sabbath observance, circumcision and the kosher diet, the principal outward signs of their once Jewish origins. Their own concept of bodily purity focussed on the sexual; they were puritanical about sex outside of marriage and even nudity was abhorred; they esteemed celibacy and sexual abstinence. They derived these sexual excesses mainly from their philosophical experiments, in the centuries before Constantine, with Neoplatonism, a revival of Platonic teaching under Plotinus (204/5-270 CE). Neoplatonists believed in the superiority of the soul over the body, and rejected sexual excesses. Christians were, by comparison with both contemporary Romans and Jews, sexual ascetics.

During these times of comparative peace, the Bishops of Rome controlled the Christian life of the capital; they also attempted to influence other bishops outside of Rome and even to interfere in their rule.

By the fourth century CE, there were political problems within the Roman Empire. There had been attempts to stabilise the structure of the Empire by dividing authority among four rulers instead of a single emperor. This experiment begun by Diocletian proved to be divisive and unwieldy. Constantine had come to power in 312 CE with a co-emperor and endeavoured to return to a central control by one emperor over all Roman possessions. For this to work, he needed a stability factor which he found in Christianity and its mental attributes. First, he recognised Christianity as a *religio licita*, a legitimate religion within the Roman Empire, and next he bestowed on it highly favourable treatment. He and the reigning

Popes, Miltiades and then Sylvester I, forged an Emperor-Pope relationship within which they were very much the junior partners. Constantine did not actually convert to Christianity until just before his death.

However, Constantine had been subsequently dismayed to discover that his new Christian territories were ideologically split over a religious debate (led mainly by a priest Arius who disputed the divinity of Jesus), just when the Empire needed religious unity. Constantine arrogantly convoked and enforced a council of Church leaders to meet at Nicaea in Asia Minor in 325 CE to resolve this conflict over the humanity and divinity of Jesus. For the most part it was the bishops from the Eastern Roman Empire who attended. Pope Sylvester I did not attend; he was represented by two legates. Constantine himself presided at the Council (at least in name, perhaps with his trusted Eusebius actually sitting for him), and Arius and his followers were condemned: Jesus was both fully human and fully divine at the same time, the official doctrine of Nicaea proclaimed.

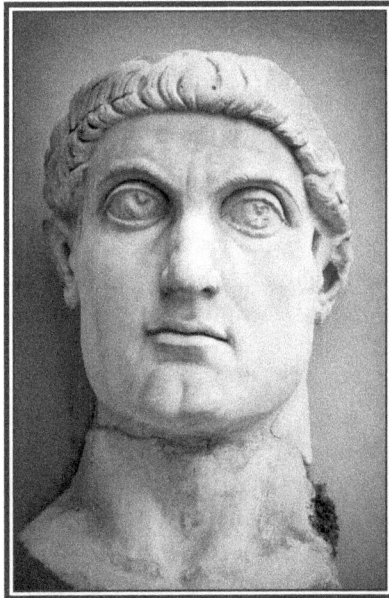

*Figure 9*
*Statue of Constantine*

Constantine left Rome for his New Rome, Constantinople, in 324. The Popes thereafter took possession of Rome. They built huge churches, many of them on the sites of previous humble house-churches. The Church Story more and more found its centre in the capital. The Scriptures were translated into Latin by order of the Pope. The Popes saw themselves more in the mould of a Roman Emperor, the Patriarchs of the West, at least on a par with the Patriarchs of the East, although they also claimed the special prestige of descending from Peter.

In 391 CE, another Roman emperor, Theodosius, went much further than Constantine. He prohibited all religious ritual other than Christianity and closed all temples other than Christian churches throughout the Empire. Greek temples, Roman temples, Egyptian temples and other religious centres were all closed. Judaism was still allowed to be practised but there was to be no further Jewish evangelism. Christianity became the official religion of the Roman Empire and displaced all others, including the imperial Roman religion.

In 431 CE the bishops of the Christian church came together once more in the city of Ephesus, where another Council considered yet another version of the Church teaching on Jesus. Nestorius (died 451), the Patriarch of Constantinople, had suggested that there was a divine Jesus and a separate human Jesus in the one person, the Virgin Mary being the mother only of the human Jesus. His teaching was rejected and Nestorius was deposed as Patriarch and exiled. Ephesus decided that there was only one 'Jesus' and Mary was mother of both the divine and human person who made up that Jesus. Mary, the Mother of God (in Greek, *Theotokos*) became the rallying call of orthodox Christian belief.

In another attempt to clear up the matter Eutyches (380-456 CE), who had been a virulent opponent of Nestorius, despite the fact that he was a presbyter under him in Constantinople, went in the opposite direction in 448 CE and stressed the unity of Jesus. He claimed that the human nature of Jesus had been absorbed into the divine nature. This was also rejected.

This struggle of minds was over the Church's interpretation of the Literary Jesus, even if the theologians of the time thought they were dealing with the Historical Jesus. The gospels were ambivalent: Jesus ate, slept and seemed to have human emotions; however, he also worked miracles, cured the sick and rose from the dead. How was Jesus to be depicted in the Church Story? The Bishop of Rome, Leo (440-461), summed up what was considered to be the orthodox teaching of the time. Whether he was imposing a solution, or simply voicing what the common opinion of the time was, is a debated question. His solution, that Jesus was fully God and fully human and yet there was only one single *hypostasis* (the underlying state or substance, in Greek philosophy, later translated into

Latin as *persona*), was accepted as the orthodox position and was ratified by the Council held at Chalcedon in 451 CE.

*We, then, following the holy Fathers, all with one consent, teach people to confess one and the same Son, our Lord Jesus Christ, the same perfect in Godhead and also perfect in humanity;*

*truly God and truly human, of a rational soul and body;*

*of the same substance with the Father according to the Godhead, and of the same substance with us according to Humanity;*

*in all things like unto us, without sin;*

*begotten before all ages of the Father according to the Godhead, and in these latter days, for us and for our salvation, born of the Virgin Mary, the Mother of God, according to humanity;*

*one and the same Christ, Son, Lord, only begotten, to be acknowledged in two natures, inconfusedly, unchangeably, indivisibly, inseparably;*

*the distinction of natures being by no means taken away by the union, but rather the property of each nature being preserved, and concurring in one Person and one Subsistence, not parted or divided into two persons, but one and the same Son, and only begotten God, the Word, the Lord Jesus Christ;*

*as the prophets from the beginning have declared concerning Him, and the Lord Jesus Christ Himself has taught us, and the Creed of the holy Fathers has handed down to us.*

This complex Chalcedonian statement was carefully worded so as to take issue with all the 'false' opinions expressed by Arius, Nestorius and Eutyches. The statement is meaningless unless the 'false' propositions are first understood in their context. With some exceptions, this statement is the solution to how the Church Story had finally interpreted the Literary Jesus in the gospels. This expanded and, for modern readers, largely incomprehensible form of the Literary Jesus has come down to the Christian churches and is officially accepted by them today. Too often it is confused with the Historical Jesus.

The Western Roman Empire, which had supported the spread of the Christian church, was eventually to implode in the fifth century. The immediate cause was a series of invasions from Germanic tribes, whom the Romans knew as 'barbarians'. Romulus Augustus was the last Western Emperor, a puppet set up by the barbarians themselves and then deposed by them in 476. But the Roman Empire had been decaying for quite some time.

In this time of decay, there had been a growing feeling, mostly in the Western Church, that the bishop of Rome had a spiritual leadership over all Christians and that his teaching, as compared to other bishops' teachings, especially reflected the original teaching of Peter and The Twelve. The basis for this acceptance of the priority of the Roman bishop was the Church Story: Peter had been nominated in the gospels by Jesus as his successor and the guardian of Christian teaching; he had come to Rome as the founder of its Christian Church and died there; the Popes in Rome were therefore in the direct line of authority from Peter. This realisation had taken some centuries to be determined.

Such was the situation of the Papacy, who continued to be elected by the Roman clergy, as the Roman Empire collapsed and Europe was thrown into turmoil.

To make sense of this period it is necessary to revert to the scheme that was derived from phenomenology of religion. Certainly by the time of the final version of the Gospel of John, Jesus was seen as a divine being. The original structure of Christianity would have looked like this:

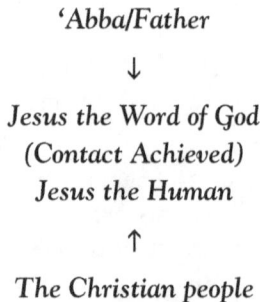

'*Abba/Father*

↓

*Jesus the Word of God*
*(Contact Achieved)*
*Jesus the Human*

↑

*The Christian people*

*But how could the one being be both an Other-worldly Intermediary and a This-worldly Intermediary? That was the whole point of the discussion between Arius, Nestorius and Eutyches and their co-religionists. By the time of Constantine, that discussion was taking a new turn. Who was the successor to Jesus the Human? Constantine exalted Peter as that successor. Hence, at the time of Constantine the only orthodox form of Christianity that was recognized was structured as follows:*

'Abba/Father

↓

Jesus the Word of God
(Contact Achieved)
Peter (and the succeeding Popes)

↑

The Christian people

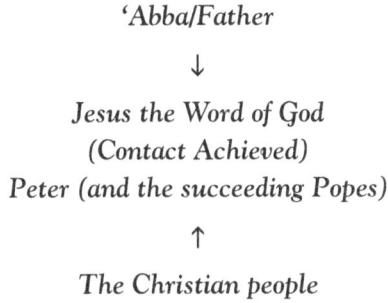

Constantine gave a new stature to the Pope, although he saw himself as politically superior to him. 'Peter' and the Popes now became the Vicars of Christ, the successors to the Human Jesus. This was the first shape taken by the Papacy: a Vicar of Christ and a successor to Peter who thereby imparts and upholds the true teaching that came from Peter and The Twelve. The Papal This-worldly Intermediary was a guaranteed teacher, and that teaching could bring salvation to humans, which simply means contact would be achieved with Ultimacy.

The establishment of the Papacy did not take place immediately, if history is taken into account. It was only over centuries that anything like a Pope as This-worldly Intermediary can be recognised. The Church Story is different: Peter was the first Pope and all other successors in an unbroken line derived their authority over all Christians from him. The Basilica of Saint Peter in Rome is the living commemoration of the primacy of Peter over The Twelve, over the Church in Rome and over the entire Church. None of this is historically verified; yet, it is all part of an important Church Story.

As the barbarian invasions changed the West, this spiritual authority of the Pope remained the only lasting institution with real authority. The people of Rome and its environs looked to the reigning Pope for protection not only for their religious solace but also for their physical welfare and protection.

From that time the Pope would gradually claim jurisdiction over the Church in an ever clearer way.

# NOTES

It is no easy matter to obtain a reliable list of Popes and their dates. There is doubt, even in the most orthodox sources, as to the exact succession of Popes. Some are listed as Pope in one source and Antipope (or illegal contender) in another. The list used in this book does not include these uncertainties. The list is dependent on the following:

Herbermann, C. et al. eds. (1905-1913), *The Catholic Encyclopedia*, RAC: New York. This is now available online.

(2012), 'I Sommi Pontifici Romani' in *Annuario Pontificio*, Libreria Vaticana: Rome. This is the Catholic Church's official list, but it includes some anomalies.

Kelly, J. (1986), *Oxford Dictionary of the Popes*, OUP: Oxford

There are a myriad number of histories of the early spread of Christianity. It would not be feasible to list them all. Two recent, interesting volumes are:

Stark, R. (2007), *Cities of God. The Real Story of How Christianity became an Urban Movement and Conquered Rome*, Harper One: New York

Ekelund, R. and Tollison, R. (2011), *Economic Origins of Roman Christianity*, University of Chicago Press: Chicago and London

# 6/
# THE POPES OF
# THE MEDIEVAL CHURCH

*The collapse of the Western Roman Empire left the Eastern Empire, with its capital in Constantinople, as the sole remnant of the great worldwide Roman Empire. It would be known as the Byzantine Empire and survive for another thousand years until Ottoman Turks took it over in 1453.*

*The period from the fall of Rome until the fall of Constantinople is generally and broadly known as the Middle Ages. It encompassed some of the great movements of thought in world history. It also encompassed some low points that we will investigate further: the Investiture Controversy, the final split between Eastern and Western Christianity and the Crusades led by Western Christians.*

*We will see how the Papacy coped with this time of drastic change and itself changed in the process. From the Constantinian Church we move first to what became known as the Byzantine Papacy and then to the Frankish Papacy.*

## The Byzantine Papacy

Justinian I (482-565) was elected as the Byzantine Emperor in Constantinople in 527. His reign would be the highpoint of the Byzantine Empire, which encompassed almost all the West Mediterranean coast. His mandate was to restore the greatness of the Eastern Empire and to regain the West. In 537 he had his own cathedral built in Constantinople, Hagia Sophia. It was meant to outshine Saint Peter's in Rome.

From 535 until 554 he was involved in wars with the Goths who had taken over much of the Empire. These wars included two campaigns in Italy; Rome was deeply involved. In 546 the Goths took the city and a great deal of destruction followed, including desecration of Saint Peter's. Then the Byzantines intervened and regained Rome the following year only to be themselves ousted in 550. However, by 552 Rome was again in Byzantine hands.

This Byzantine occupation was to usher in an extraordinary era in Papal history when the Popes were under the political control of the Eastern Empire. They were answerable in all things to the Byzantine Emperor. The reigning Popes from the time of Justinian onwards were as follows:

✝ Felix III (II) (483-92)
✝ Gelasius I (492-96)
✝ Anastasius II (496-98)
✝ Symmachus (498-514)
✝ Hormisdas (514-23)
✝ John I (523-26)
✝ Felix IV (sometimes counted as III) (526-30)
✝ Boniface II (530-32)
✝ John II (533-35)
✝ Agapetus I (535-36). Also called Agapitus I
✝ Silverius (536-37)
✝ Vigilius (537–555)
✝ Pelagius I (556–561)
✝ John III (561–574)
✝ Benedict I (575–579)
✝ Pelagius II (579–590)

✞ Gregory I (the Great) (590–604)

✞ Sabinian (604–606)

✞ Boniface III (607)

✞ Boniface IV (608–615)

✞ Adeodatus I (615–618)

✞ Boniface V (619–625)

✞ Honorius I (625–638)

✞ Severinus (640)

✞ John IV (640–642)

✞ Theodore I (642–649)

✞ Martin I (649–653)

✞ Eugene I (654–657)

Justinian desperately wanted religious unity in his Empire. To fulfill this aim, he forced the reigning Pope, Silverius, to resign in 537 and, in his place, he himself appointed first Vigilius and then Pelagius I without any consultation. From this time onwards, he required that the name of any new Pope be submitted to the Byzantine Emperor for prior approval. This could mean lengthy delays before a Pope was consecrated, sometimes up to a year.

These Popes were Greek speakers, combining the traditions of East and West. None of them could question the authority of the Emperor in Constantinople. This would remain standard practice for more than a century: 537 until 752. In 553 a Council was held in Constantinople which demanded that nothing within the Church could be enacted that went counter to the command of the Emperor. The Pope in Rome meekly accepted this requirement. He had little option. Rome was a ruin. Its population by around the year 500 would only have been 30,000 (down from 800,000 a hundred years earlier). The people had to endure living amid the destroyed glory of a past age, with dismal swamps producing malarial infection.

It was only with Gregory I (590-604 CE) that the Papacy asserted any independence from the Empire. He came from a wealthy Roman family. They had holdings on the Caelian Hill in Rome. At some time he had converted his family's sumptuous home into a monastery, where he himself lived the life of a contemplative monk. Then, he was selected to go as Ambassador to Constantinople, where he became involved in international politics. From this position he was elected Pope. He set out to energise the Roman Church. He not only commissioned Augustine of Canterbury to go to England to convert the Angles, but also promoted missionary activity in the Netherlands and Germany.

In 595 CE he stated, with regard to his own understanding of the Papacy, that

> … the care of the whole Church has been committed to the blessed Peter, Prince of the Apostles. Behold he received the keys of the kingdom of heaven; to him was given the power of binding and loosing, to him the care and principate of the whole Church was committed.

This did not mean that the Popes defied the patronage of the Byzantine Empire. Because of their fidelity to the Eastern Emperor, the Roman Popes were looked upon with increasing favour. So, in 607 Boniface III was able to obtain from the Emperor a decree describing Rome as 'the head of all the Churches'. The Pope was gaining in pre-eminence and Popes came and went without any great problems. There was a turnover: ten Popes in the first half of the seventh century.

But there would eventually be dissent. Martin I (649-653) refused to obtain Byzantine approval for his election. Within a year he called a Council at the Lateran to discuss a particular heresy, Monothelitism. The issue itself is an arcane debate as to whether Jesus had one will or two, a human one and a divine one, by which he made decisions. In the scheme of things, it was of very little importance to the populace. However, the then Eastern Emperor, Constans II, had already issued a decree that any discussion on Monothelitism had to cease, since it was causing political strife in his Empire between those who upheld and those who denied the two wills theory.

Martin reported to him that Monothelitism should be condemned and that the Emperor's own decree should be rescinded. The Emperor was furious at his underling, Martin, dictating to him. The latter was abducted from Rome and taken to Constantinople for a trial related to his audacious calling of the Council. He was found guilty and exiled to the Crimea where he died. Even before his death, another Pope was elected in Rome and he did request imperial approval, Eugene I.

✟ Vitalian (657–672)
✟ Adeodatus II (672–676)
✟ Donus (676–678)
✟ Agatho (678–681)

✝ Leo II (682–683)
✝ Benedict II (684–685)
✝ John V (685–686)
✝ Conon (686–687)
✝ Sergius I (687–701)

From the time of Eugene I until Conon (686-687), the Popes obeyed the Emperor in Constantinople to the letter and the friction between the Empire and the Papacy lessened.

During the reign of Pope Vitalian, the Eastern Emperor Constans II came to Rome, most probably to organise military attacks on some warring groups of Slavs and Lombards. He was received with great ceremony by the Pope and people and much wealth was stripped from Rome's buildings, together with other ornamentation, for him to take back for his constructions in Constantinople. However, he was murdered after leaving Rome and Vitalian refused to recognise his murderer as the new Emperor. He supported Constans' son, Constantine IV.

His choice proved wise. Constantine IV eventually gained the throne and, out of gratitude, showered honours on Vitalian. While Donus was Pope, Constantine IV convoked a Third Council in Constantinople in 680 CE and a request was sent for the Pope to send a submission; by this time, Donus was dead and Agatho elected. He was a Greek from Sicily.

Pope Agatho (678-681) commissioned groups of clerics to debate Monothelitism throughout Italy. Then he sent a representative with his formal statement condemning it. This was accepted. The Council finally abandoned the heresy and the Church returned to the statement on Jesus from the Council of Chalcedon.

In subsequent negotiations, the Emperor handed the city of Ravenna, which had been an Eastern possession, back to Rome and lessened taxes on the Papacy. From that time the Exarch of Ravenna (the Emperor's representative) would be permitted to approve the selection of a Pope rather than going to the Emperor.

A new period of East-West harmony began.

However, the harmony established by Constans II and Constantine IV would not last. Justinian II convoked a Council (called the *Quinisext Council*[23]) in 692, during the time of Pope Sergius I, that was ignored by the Western bishops and the Pope himself. This Council passed decrees which were then forwarded to the Pope with a demand for their acceptance. Sergius I objected to this procedure. In particular, he would not accept decrees calling for any liberalisation of the requirement for clerical celibacy (which was not required in the Eastern Church and, while not a strict rule in the West, was being imposed in some areas), nor the prohibitions against eating blood-foods or using the Lamb of God as a sacred image of Jesus.[24]

- ✠ John VI (701–705)
- ✠ John VII (705–707)
- ✠ Sisinnius (708)
- ✠ Constantine (708–715)
- ✠ Gregory II (715–731)
- ✠ Gregory III (731–741)
- ✠ Zachary (741–752)

This rift was not healed until 710 CE when Justinian II ordered Pope Constantine (708-715) to come to Constantinople and he meekly complied, bringing a party of mainly Greek clergy to the audience. Peace returned to the Christian world, but this was to be the last journey of a Pope to Constantinople until Paul VI visited modern Istanbul to bring a message of reconciliation in 1967.

The Church Story in this period had taken a new turn. The Eastern Empire saw itself as the Kingdom of God on earth; it claimed to be the very centre of civilisation with its arts, technology and knowledge. It was ruled by the Emperor who claimed to be the Vicar of God on earth (and thereby claimed at the same time that the Pope was not!) although he did recognise that Rome and its Pope had a very important status. The earlier Byzantine Papacy would have agreed with the Church Story, perhaps with some refinements. Yet, in the eighth century this understanding started to unravel.

The main issue was strangely what has become known as iconoclasm (the breaking of religious images). Basing themselves on the Jewish prohibition of worshipping images, the iconoclasts (image-breakers) in the Eastern Church rejected the use of images of Jesus, the Virgin Mary and saints in Christian worship. This was no small matter. Images had been revered as, in some way, directing the spiritual power of the person depicted (whether the person was Jesus, the Virgin Mary or a saint) towards the faithful people who honoured the images; for many, they were essential to spiritual wellbeing.

When Leo III succeeded as Emperor of Constantinople in 717, by forcing the abdication of Theodosius III, he was first confronted by an advancing army of Umayyad Muslims. Having defeated them, he turned his mind to religious matters and sided with the iconoclasts. The use of images was forbidden.

This religious stance caused consternation throughout East and West. Popes Gregory II (715-731) and Gregory III (731-741) protested vociferously. After all, Rome depended hugely on images for pilgrims and for trade. Gregory III called a Synod at which all iconoclasts were declared excommunicated. Iconoclasm also brought about revolution in Greece and the definitive breakaway of Ravenna from the Emperor's control. Leo III took it badly. He retaliated and removed many areas previously belonging to the Pope from Roman control. What this really meant was that Rome and the Pope were being cast out of the Eastern Empire. In 741 Pope Zachary was elected as the last Greek Pope, and the last to seek confirmation of his election from the Greek powers.

The 'Byzantine Papacy' was thereby concluded; the Empire now had its own problems with Islam and with religious unrest at home. The Pope would have to look to the West for any political or military help.

So, the Popes turned to the West and lost contact with the East.

### The Frankish Papacy

&#10013; Stephen III (752-57)
&#10013; Paul I (757-67)
&#10013; Stephen IV (767-72)
&#10013; Adrian I (772-95)
&#10013; Leo III (795-816)
&#10013; Stephen V (816-17)
&#10013; Paschal I (817-24)
&#10013; Eugene II (824-27)
&#10013; Valentine (827)
&#10013; Gregory IV (827-44)
&#10013; Sergius II (844-47)
&#10013; Leo IV (847-55)
&#10013; Benedict III (855-58)
&#10013; Nicholas I (the Great) (858-67)
&#10013; Adrian II (867-72)
&#10013; John VIII (872-82)
&#10013; Marinus I (882-84)

✝ Adrian III (884-85)

✝ Stephen VI (885-91)

✝ Formosus (891-96)

✝ Boniface VI (896)

✝ Stephen VII (896-97)

✝ Romanus (897)

✝ Theodore II (897)

✝ John IX (898-900)

✝ Benedict IV (900-03)

✝ Leo V (903)

✝ Sergius III (904-11)

✝ Anastasius III (911-13)

✝ Lando (913-14)

✝ John X (914-28)

✝ Leo VI (928)

✝ Stephen VIII (929-31)

✝ John XI (931-35)

✝ Leo VII (936-39)

✝ Stephen IX (939-42)

✝ Marinus II (942-46)

✝ Agapetus II (946-55)

✝ John XII (955-63)

✝ Leo VIII (963-64)

✝ Benedict V (964)

✝ John XIII (965-72)

✝ Benedict VI (973-74)

✝ Benedict VII (974-83)

✝ John XIV (983-84)

✝ John XV (985-96)

✝ Gregory V (996-99)

✝ Sylvester II (999-1003)

✝ John XVII (1003)

✝ John XVIII (1003-09)

✝ Sergius IV (1009-12)

Since 568 CE Italy had been infiltrated by the Lombards. Migrating probably from Scandinavia to seek new lands, the Lombards arrived into the German area and eventually settled near the Danube around modern Austria. There they would be joined by other nomad groups and they decided to move south into Italy. Their invasion was almost unopposed. They established a Lombard Kingdom in Italy that would remain in place until 774 CE.

Because of the weak position of Rome, at odds with the Eastern Empire, Pope Stephen III (752-757) knew that he could expect no further help from there and so he travelled to the new Frankish king, Pepin the Younger. Pepin heard his case and invaded Italy and cleared the Lombards at least from the area around the kingdom of Ravenna.

This intervention must be put into context.

Sometime in the eighth century a forged document was circulated and it put the Pope centre-stage in Italy. It was called The *Donation of Constantine*. It purported to explain how Constantine, back in the fourth century, had been baptized by the reigning Bishop of Rome, Sylvester I, and that, in gratitude for being cured of leprosy, Constantine had handed over his entire civil possessions in Italy to the Pope. The Pope was by Roman law, according to the *Donation*, a civil ruler.[25]

Pepin probably believed that the forged *Donation of Constantine* was a valid document and that he was bound to honour it. He gave control of much of central Italy, from Rome to Ravenna, to the Pope. This action was important; it definitively marked the end of the Byzantine Papacy and it marked the beginning of a Frankish Papacy. It was also the beginning of the Papal States over which the Pope would have command, as if he were a civil ruler, until 1870. The political history of Europe and the Papacy would become even more entangled.

However, the Lombards still continued to cause trouble and during the next two centuries they menaced Rome again. A very active and long-reigning Pope, Adrian I (772-795), once more called on the Franks and in 772 the king of the Franks, Charlemagne, son of the deceased Pepin, defeated the Lombards permanently and annexed their lands to his own. Charlemagne would rule for forty-seven years (768-814). He was an extraordinary ruler, able to introduce efficient administration that would maintain his new holdings. He admired Rome and its architecture. He also wanted to maintain the Christian Church of Rome.

The following Pope, Leo III (795-816), still feeling unsafe in Rome, requested Charlemagne to come to the city in 800. Leo slyly arranged a ceremony in Saint Peters, on the pretext of anointing Charlemagne's son as his heir. However, he took the opportunity to crown Charlemagne as Emperor (despite the fact that the Emperor was supposed to reside in Constantinople). Charlemagne adopted the title of 'Charles, most serene Augustus, crowned by God, great and pacific emperor, governing the Roman Empire'. There was now an alliance of Pope and Emperor of the Romans. This was seen as replacing the Roman Empire that had ground to a halt in the fifth century. However, for the Byzantines this was all sheer heresy. The Pope, as far as the Byzantines were concerned, had abandoned the path of true Christian teaching.

However, after Charlemagne died in 814 there was disruption. Charlemagne had brought the Church under his protection. The Roman Pope, bishops and priests were civil servants. His son Louis succeeded him but soon the new Roman Empire was divided. There were many seeking to be Emperor and there were warlords who claimed to rule local areas within the Empire.

*Figure 10*
*Holy Roman Empire*

The prestige of the Papacy meantime had reached a very low ebb. It was the play-thing of the great Roman families. Having one's own Pope in Rome meant political dominance. Perhaps the best indication of this was the Cadaver Synod in 897. Stephen VII (896-897), sometimes numbered as Stephen VI, hated Formosus who had been Pope before Stephen's predecessor. Stephen had been elected because of the patronage of the House of Spoleto and the people of Spoleto claimed that Formosus had unjustly rejected their claimant for the position of the Holy Roman Emperor. Stephen had the corpse of Formosus exhumed, dressed it in Papal finery and placed it on a throne set up in the Basilica of John Lateran. Charges were laid – of perjury and worse. He was sentenced accordingly, had his fingers mutilated (those of his blessing hand) and then the mummified corpse was thrown in the Tiber.

Perhaps the most corrupt of all the Popes during this time was John XII (955-963) and reflects the low ebb of this period. Alberic II was the secular ruler of Rome. He appointed five Popes in a row and then demanded that his own son, Octavian, be appointed Pope. So at eighteen years of age, Octavian became Pope John XII. He had no religious interest and no competence to be Pope. At the age of twenty-seven he had a stroke while in bed with a married woman.

After there had been much loss of Papal territories to petty rulers, Otto I (936-973) invaded Italy, making it a part of the Empire in 962, after being crowned by the Pope. After his death once more local Italian families established their own dynasties and set up their own Popes in Rome.

What was the Papacy after this interlude of protection by the Holy Roman Empire? The Popes were no more than local Italian prince-bishops, subordinated to the rule of Roman families. Yet throughout the Western world there was general agreement that the Pope was the guardian of great spiritual treasures. Whether he was good or evil made little difference. Foreigners still made the unsafe journey to Rome to see the city of Peter's successor and to glimpse perhaps 'Peter'.

✟ Benedict VIII (1012-24)
✟ John XIX (1024-32)
✟ Benedict IX (1032-45)26
✟ Sylvester III (1045)
✟ Benedict IX (1045)

✟ Gregory VI (1045-46)

✟ Clement II (1046-47)

✟ Benedict IX (1047-48)

✟ Damasus II (1048)

✟ Leo IX (1049-54)

The dire situation of these Supreme Pontiffs can be gauged by the fact that when the Emperor Henry III, Holy Roman Emperor from 1039 to 1046, came to Rome he found three Popes in dispute: Gregory VI, Sylvester III and Benedict IX. This was because the institution had come, as stated above, under the control of powerful families in Rome and each had their own following.

Benedict IX was actually Pope three times: 1032-1044, 1045, 1047-8. He was arguably the most corrupt Pope ever (but he did have competitors!). Elected at the age of ten or twelve, with the help of bribery by his father, Count Alberic II of Tusculum, he spent a decade of sinful and decadent rule before he was deposed by the Crescenti family, one of the power players in Rome, and exiled. He then excommunicated his successor, Sylvester III, and returned to be Pope with the help of his father's private army.

However, two months later he sold the Papacy to his godfather, Giovanni Graziano, who took the name of Gregory VI. Rumour was that Benedict needed money to get married. He soon regretted this action and changed his mind. He reappeared in Rome, so that there were at that time the three Popes in Rome who confronted Henry III: Benedict IX, Sylvester III and Gregory VI.

Henry III, solved the problem by deposing the three of them at the Synod of Sutri in 1046. He declared, in fact, that no cleric in Rome at that time was worthy of appointment and selected his own candidate, Clement II (1046-1047). Clement died within a year, possibly being poisoned. The irrepressible Benedict took the opportunity to install himself once more. Henry III would have none of it and deposed him in favour of his own choice, Damasus II (1048), but poor Damasus II lasted only twenty-three days (and poison was again suspected).[27]

Henry III then appointed Leo IX (1049-1054). Leo would only accept the Emperor's nomination after the clergy and people of Rome ratified it. He was an able Pope and bent on reforming the Church in challenging times. His reign changed the dire direction taken by the Papacy at the time. Corruption was attacked; bishops involved in the sale of spiritual goods were deposed; the appointment of bishops by secular rulers was condemned. However, his enthusiasm to protect the Papacy angered the Byzantines when he led military attacks against the Normans in south Italy. They regarded this as their territory, not that of the Bishop of Rome. This would be a factor leading to a Schism with the Eastern Church.

✞ Victor II (1055-57)

✞ Stephen X (1057-58)

✞ Nicholas II (1058-61)

✞ Alexander II (1061-73)

✞ Gregory VII (1073-85)

✞ Victor III (1086-87)

✞ Urban II (1088-99)

✞ Paschal II (1099-1118)

✞ Gelasius II (1118-19)

✞ Callistus II (1119-24)

✞ Honoris II (1124-30)

✞ Innocent II (1130-43)

✞ Celestine II (1143-44)

✞ Lucius II (1144-45)

✞ Eugene III (1145-53)

✞ Anastasius IV (1153-54)

✞ Adrian IV (1154-59)

✞ Alexander III (1159-81)

✞ Lucius III (1181-85)

✞ Urban III (1185-87)

✞ Gregory VIII (1187)

✞ Clement III (1187-91)

✞ Celestine III (1191-98)

✞ Innocent III (1198-1216)

✞ Honorius III (1216-27)

✞ Gregory IX (1227-41)

✞ Celestine IV (1241)

✞ Innocent IV (1243-54)

✞ Alexander IV (1254-61)

✞ Urban IV (1261-64)

✞ Clement IV (1265-68)

✝ Gregory X (1271-76)

✝ Innocent V (1276)

✝ Adrian V (1276)

✝ John XXI (1276-77)

✝ Nicholas III (1277-80)

✝ Martin IV (1281-85)

Leo's reforms did not end the Papal problems. By the mid-eleventh century the Church had come under lay rule. The dioceses under their bishops and monasteries under their abbots had become corporations controlling huge finances and land-holdings. Hence, there was a temptation for rulers to control the election of bishops and abbots, as well as the election of the Pope. Local rulers saw the need to curb these powerful enclaves and they did so.

Another issue in the Roman Church was clerical celibacy. In the East, only bishops were required to be celibate (if married prior to becoming a bishop, they had to separate from their wives). In the West the provision, although it came into force gradually and sporadically, applied to all deacons, priests and bishops. This was a strange rule. Celibacy (like poverty) was the domain of the monks, not priests. Monks chose to be poor and celibate. Priestly marriage was at first common. The eleventh century saw vociferous calls for an imposition of clerical celibacy. Earlier, under Benedict VIII, there had been a demand that priests not marry, but his motivation was that Church lands and goods were being handed on from priestly father to his children.

However, in the eleventh century, the motivation was the provision of a ritually clean priesthood. The grounds for this were a growing taboo on sex: the human body was defiled and clouded the mind and soul in the sexual act. This call for celibacy was reinforced by the development of the teaching on transubstantiation – that the bread and wine during the Mass really became the flesh and blood of Jesus. For a priest who might have been intimate with a woman (who menstruated, suckled and was of the earth) it seemed most improper that he should thereafter handle the consecrated species.

This repudiation of sex for priests had been part of the reform movement of Leo IX.

The wider spirit of reform continued. It brought with it dramatic changes including several phases: The Investiture Controversy, the Schism with the East and the Crusades.

## The Investiture Controversy

As we have seen the appointment of Popes and bishops had gradually been removed from the hands of the ecclesiastical leaders. In the early centuries the process of election of the Pope followed the custom of the time whereby the local Roman community, by means of their clergy, made the choice. Then, as life in Rome became more complex, the Emperors had intervened and ensured that all was done in an orderly fashion and to their satisfaction. Next, as we have seen, the selection required approval from the Eastern Emperor.

In turn, Frankish Emperors saw part of their role as Pope-makers. This system did not last and local family leaders in Italy became the electors. Further, rulers within Italy considered it their prerogative to appoint bishops and abbots in their own lands as well as Popes. The Church wanted to regain its independence to elect its own Bishop of Rome and its own bishops and abbots. The issue was control. The Church saw itself as controlled by laypeople and by feudal families. A confrontation between Papal power and civil power had come to boiling point.

This confrontation reached its high point when Gregory VII (1073-1085) resisted the demands of the Holy Roman Emperor, Henry IV. Gregory made it clear that only the Pope had the universal power to rule. In his *Dictatus Papae* published in 1075 Gregory put forward twenty-seven propositions regarding the Pope. Papal power, he stated, came directly from God and could not be challenged by any other person. He turned the tables: the Pope should not only appoint bishops but he could appoint civil leaders; and, importantly and threateningly, he could depose them. Henry IV was outraged by the very suggestion. He replied and headed his Letter:

> Henry, king not through usurpation but through the holy ordination of God, to Hildebrand (the secular name of Gregory VII), at present not Pope but false monk.

In other words, Henry saw his kingship as coming from God and he was answerable to God alone. Henry then called for a new Papal election and addressed the Pope:

> I, Henry, king by the grace of God, with all of my Bishops, say to you, come down, come down, and be damned throughout the ages.

But Gregory VII fearlessly pressed ahead. He demanded a meeting with the Emperor, who realised that he had lost popular support throughout his holdings and, according to the story, Gregory made him wait outside a castle in Canossa in frigid conditions. He then absolved the broken man from his sinfulness. The story may be legendary, but it reflects the reality of the conflict between Pope and Emperor.

Gregory VII made his idea of the Papacy clear. He was a successor to Peter. But that was not sufficient. Other bishops could trace their lineage back to The Twelve. As Pope he claimed to be the successor of Peter and therefore the successor of Jesus. In the next century one of the Popes, Innocent III (1198-1216), would write in this vein:

> We are the successor of the prince of the Apostles, but we are not his vicar, not the vicar of any man or Apostle, but the vicar of Jesus Christ himself.

After Gregory VII, the Concordat of Worms in 1122, a Council agreed to by Pope Calixtus II and Henry V, seemed to solve the conflict: only the Pope can appoint bishops. However, in reality the issue was to remain unresolved for a long time.

This gave rise to a remarkable turnabout during the latter period of the Middle Ages. In debating the Investiture Controversy, the claim was made that the Pope was superior not only over any religious power but over any secular power; Emperors and other civil leaders only had their authority because of the agreement of the Pope to bestow it. This meant that the Church, the Christian people identical at that time more or less with society at large, should be governed by the Pope and the clergy and that secular leaders only ruled with the assent of the Church. The tables had turned since the Byzantine Papacy when the Pope was the Eastern Emperor's vassal and the Frankish Papacy when the Holy Roman Emperor controlled the election and the lamentable period when petty families and rulers appointed Popes. The Pope at this time was considered by many, including himself, as not only the spiritual ruler of Christians but superior in authority to all secular rulers who owed him obedience.

By the time of Innocent III (1198-1216) the Papacy claimed to be rulers of the world. For example, seeing the rise of the Cathars in France and Spain, dissidents who like the earlier Gnostics claimed that Jesus had been God only and disdained the flesh and dismissed the organised Church, the Papacy sent its own Crusade to destroy them. They were social misfits in a world that should be orthodox Christian.

As a result the Church required that Pope, bishops and abbots should be elected by Church officials only and that secular rulers should have no say in such elections. Reform was in the air since secular rulers had grown used to controlling church offices and there had even been a trade in them. The ruling clique in Western Europe accepted all of this grudgingly but sometimes continued to question the idea of the supreme authority of the Pope.

The Popes now saw themselves as the successor of Peter and also of Constantine. Hence the Papal coronation became a secular event with royal robes and a distinctive crown. According to the forged *Donation of Constantine*, the crown or tiara symbolised the Pope's authority over the Western world.[28]

With the increased power of the Pope, the election process was further refined, since it had to be seen as transparent. Gregory X (1271-1276) established the Conclave (*con clave* in Latin, 'with a key'). For an election the cardinals would be placed in a locked hall, having no contact with the outside world until there was an election, thus ensuring secrecy and no opportunity for bribery.

Alongside this battle between Church and State, from which the Papacy emerged victorious, there was another between East and West.

### *East and West Finally Divide*

As we have seen, there had always been a division between the East and the West within the Christian Church. The East had retained the Christian Scriptures in Greek while the West had translated them into Latin, and there were consequently some differences in the texts due to the different manuscripts preferred by each. In argument, each side's theologians supported opposing positions but sometimes on the basis of different biblical texts. Their ritual differed in external form (unleavened bread used for the Eucharist in the West, and leavened bread in the East; Confirmation became a separate sacrament in the West while it was combined with Baptism in the East). There was a difference in attitude to sacred images, as we have also seen, and there was a different understanding of the relationship of the Church to the secular authority; the Greeks were still much more subservient to their Emperors.

The Eastern Church had never accepted the supremacy of the Bishop of Rome over all its own bishops or over the Patriarch of Constantinople. There was a simmering, ongoing animosity and, during the Middle Ages, a very significant rift developed that exacerbated earlier cracks.

To review that rift we should go over a series of events, some previously covered, that had affected the situation.

- In 330, Constantine had decided to move his capital from Rome to the East and chose the fortress town of Byzantium, which he immodestly renamed Constantinople, 'the city of Constantine'. Up to this point the great centres of Christianity had been Jerusalem, Antioch, Alexandria and Rome. Constantinople was now added as a fifth centre and the Council of Constantinople in 381 CE declared that Constantinople was equal to Rome. This demoted Alexandria. The leaders of these five principal sites were called 'patriarchs' and they had the right to appoint bishops in the surrounding areas and to preside at local church councils.
- Then, the bishop of Rome began to claim a position of absolute superiority over the other four centres and their bishops, not just a position of first among equals.
- A new development was that by the seventh century CE the religion of Islam, originating in the Arabian peninsula, had taken over Jerusalem, Alexandria and Antioch. The cities were no longer under Christian rule and their importance as Christian centres quickly diminished.
- Only Rome and Constantinople remained as major Christian centres still under local Christian rule. But these two could not forge an understanding or unity. Their Christian cultures diverged more and more. The Bishop of Rome claimed universal authority; the Eastern Patriarch refused to comply.
- In 1054 CE Pope Leo IX presumptuously sent an official envoy to Constantinople to require the absolute submission of the Patriarch to himself as the supreme leader of Christianity. Leo had already angered political Constantinople by attacking the Normans in southern Italy. The Greeks still considered that area their domain. The Patriarch, as expected, refused to submit. The envoy then solemnly excommunicated the Patriarch and the Patriarch retaliated by excommunicating the Pope.

At this point it became obvious that the long and bitter separation was irreparable. The two Romes had split, and to this day they have not come back together (although the excommunications have been lifted in recent times).

Soon after this, prompted by the claims of the Roman Papacy, the haphazard way in which Popes in Rome (sometimes by vote, by acclamation, by appointment by a civil ruler) had been elected was rectified. In 1059 Pope Nicholas II published a document, *In Nomine Domini* (In the Name of the Lord), which allowed only cardinals to vote in a papal election.

Cardinals had been the early advisors to the Pope. At first the cardinals were appointed from bishops around Rome as well as priests together with deacons within the City. They were known by the Latin word for 'hinges', *cardines*. Nicholas made them Papal electors. Rules and procedures were further devised under Nicholas II, the main architect being Cardinal Hildebrand who was himself to become Gregory VII. Eugene III (1145-1153) formally constituted these electors into a College of Cardinals and they, after the death of a Pope, would enter the secret Conclave to vote a successor.

The Schism between East and West solved one festering aspect of the Papacy. The Pope, at least *de facto*, was not the ruler of the Eastern Church.

### The Crusades

The eleventh century saw a new phenomenon – the Crusades (from the French 'to take up the Cross'), a series of wars waged by European Christians in the Middle East from 1095 to 1291. In 638 Jerusalem had fallen to the Muslim Arabs under their general Omar. Jerusalem became the possession of successive Arab dynasties. A majestic mosque, the Dome of the Rock, commemorating the ascent of Muhammad into Heaven during his lifetime, was built on the presumed site of the destroyed Jewish Temple. Western Jewish and Christian pilgrims still had access to the city, since pilgrimage taxes were a thriving source of income for the Arab rulers.

However, the turning point came in 1009 when the Church of the Holy Sepulchre, built by Constantine the Great to honour the places where Jesus died and then arose from the dead, was destroyed by the Caliph Al-Hakim. This hit at the very heart of Christianity. The local Byzantine Christians in Jerusalem were allowed to rebuild the Church, but pilgrimage to Jerusalem became restricted and dangerous.

Then Alexios I, the Eastern Emperor, called upon all Christians in the world to come to the aid of the Byzantine Empire, besieged by Seljuk Turks. The whole of the East might be overrun by these Turks, it was feared. Western Christians took up the challenge.

The convocation of the First Crusade was made by Pope Urban II (1088-1099) who delivered a stirring speech in 1095 in Clermont, France, calling on Christians to arm themselves and remove the Muslims from the Holy Land and regain free access to the holy places in and around Jerusalem. He promised all participants a plenary indulgence, remission of all punishment (which would take place in Purgatory, about which more will be said below) still due to sins that had been confessed. The remission would be granted on account of the 'penance' they would undergo in fighting a Just War. In time, this was taken to mean that a soldier dying in battle went straight to heaven (which it never meant). The exact text of the speech has been lost but it had its effect. Soldiers became pilgrims who would fight their way to the Holy Land.

The Western Christian army would have numbered some two hundred thousand armed soldiers. Many of them were from the Frankish area and so were known as 'Franks'. The Muslims accordingly dubbed all Crusaders as 'Franks'. There was no unified command. European leaders simply directed their troops in the same general direction. The fact that the reigning Pope was able to convoke such a mighty army to fight the Crusades demonstrated the extent to which his temporal power had grown. The kings of Europe who answered his call led their armies at his behest. The Crusaders were the Pope's soldiers.

The First Crusade lasted between 1095 and 1099. Despite lack of coordination it was a success. The Christian army took possession of Jerusalem and the surrounding areas. They established a Kingdom of Jerusalem and three other Crusader States adjacent. It was the beginning of a new Crusader culture with its own architecture and worldview which painted the Muslim as The Enemy, the Jew as the Christ-Killer and War as a normal adjunct to a good life.

In all there would be nine Crusades, although the numbering of them differs from scholar to scholar. The earlier ones were mainly successful; the latter were mainly abject failures.

The Crusades showed that the Popes had made a claim to rule the entire world, not just his religious group, with a universal authority.

✟ Honorius IV (1285-87)
✟ Nicholas IV (1288-92)
✟ Celestine V (1294)
✟ Boniface VIII (1294-1303)
✟ Benedict XI (1303-1304)

By 1291 the Crusade adventure was over and the land reverted to Muslim rule. There had been almost a two hundred year interlude of Christian bitterly pitted against Muslim in the East. The cost was prohibitive. The Crusades gave rise to a continuing violent relationship between Christian and Muslim, a continuing violent relationship between Western Christian and Eastern Christian, a continuing violent relationship between Christian and Jew.

By this time, there were aristocratic factions at war within the boundaries of Rome, and fortresses were built in the city for protection. Popes were often enough in personal danger. They remained Bishops of Rome and claimed precedence over other bishops but they resided elsewhere. Thus, Orvieto, Perugia and Viterbo became alternative lodging places for Popes and their court. The Curia, the Papal administration, and the College of Cardinals travelled with the Popes to these outposts. When a Pope died, the Conclave was held in that place. Having the Pope present in a city might boost the city's prestige and might bring economic advantages, but there could be political dangers too for the citizens, at which point the city authorities might and did ask the Pope to move on.

Of special interest at this time was Celestine V (1294-1295), a happenstance Pope. He was a monk and hermit known as Pietro da Morrone. Having been a Benedictine, he had set up his own order of monks. After the death of Nicholas IV in 1292, the cardinals met at Perugia. There were dark politics involved and after two years and three months the Conclave had not come to a decision. Pietro sent the Conclave a fiery letter demanding that they elect a Pope immediately or else divine vengeance would come upon them all. After receiving this, the Dean of the College of Cardinals proclaimed that Pietro himself, then aged 79, would be Pope; the College quickly agreed. This was an election by proclamation.

Brought to the Conclave, Pietro at first refused the position, but cardinals and royalty persuaded him to accept and he chose the name of Celestine V. He was incompetent, possibly mentally unstable, passing inappropriate decrees and appointing cardinals at whim. He wanted, during the season of Advent, to hand over the Papacy to three cardinals, so that he could pray and fast. He was informed that this was impossible.

And so, one final decree was initiated under his papacy: the right of a Pope to resign. It was passed and he then resigned.[29] The reasons he gave for his decision were: humility, a purer life, a stainless conscience, the deficiencies of his own physical strength, his ignorance, the perverseness of the people, his longing for the tranquility of his former life.

However, he did not regain his monastic tranquility. His successor, Boniface VIII (1294-1303) was afraid that enemies would make him into a competing Antipope. Pietro was imprisoned in Fumone in Campagna. There he died nine months later; whether his death was natural or not has been a matter of speculation.

Boniface VIII, Pietro's successor, was to make the strongest assertion of supreme Papal authority, spiritual and secular. He denied all Church privileges to the French king, Philip IV, and summoned him to Rome to answer further charges. In retaliation, Philip laid his own charges against the Pope regarding simony (selling spiritual benefits for money), sodomy, sorcery and heresy. This stirred the Pope to issue the clearest statement of Papal power ever known. In 1302 he wrote an encyclical letter *Unam Sanctam* in which he attested:

> We declare, state, define and pronounce that it is altogether neces-sary to salvation for every human creature to be subject to the Roman pontiff.

This claim – that not only was the Pope the leader of the Church, leader of both Western and Eastern Christianity, but the leader of the entire world – only poured oil on the simmering fire. French troops invaded Italy and, together with some Italian forces, they arrested Boniface in Anagni which was his home town. He died several weeks later.

The excesses of Boniface VIII would lead directly to the Popes in Avignon. Having made extravagant claims, the patience of the secular European rulers with the Papacy was put to the test.

*The Papacy had become deeply involved in controversy. Not only had the Popes caused the final separation from the Eastern Church, not only challenged world civil authority, but they also became involved in the equivalent of a World War on the basis of religion in the Crusades.*

*These three significant movements – the Investiture Controversy, the Division of East and West, the Crusades – affected the Papacy deeply. The Popes hoped that possession of the Holy Land, once ruled by the Byzantines, would give them leverage in their ongoing struggle with the Patriarch of Constantinople. The Pope not the Patriarch would be the titular king of the Holy Land. At the same time, the In-vestiture Controversy had just preceded the convocation of the First Crusade. The Pope was claiming temporal power, to be the king of all kings; then, he used such power to call together the greatest army known to that time in world history. It worked – the armies marched* under his banner to Jerusalem. *The Investiture Controversy, the Division between Eastern and Western Christianity and the Crusades all became connected with a dangerous mentality.*

*They all conspired to define what the Pope meant. The successor to Peter had now become not only a religious This-worldly Intermediary but a secular ruler with the world at his feet. The Papacy had strayed from the realm of religion into that of world political power. It would take a long time for the Pope to return to the role of Intermediary.*

*Has the Papacy yet returned?*

### *The Popes in France*

*The Middle Ages continued but, towards their end, the Papacy was faced with an even greater challenge than accompanied its claim to world domination. The princes of Europe were alarmed by the growing secular power of the Papacy. They needed to rein in the rampant authority claimed by the Pope. Just when the Church seemed to be most secure and powerful, with the Pope seemingly able to dictate to all the powers in the West, there was a serious disruption that would distort the shape of the Papacy yet again. The disruption came from France.*

✝ Clement V (1305–1314)
✝ John XXII (1316–1334)
✝ Benedict XII (1334–1342)
✝ Clement VI (1342–1352)
✝ Innocent VI (1352–1362)
✝ Urban V (1362–1370)
✝ Gregory XI (1370-1378)

There had been friction between the French king, Philip IV, and the ruling Pope for some time. Philip bristled under the Papal claims that he ruled only by the pleasure of the Pope. In 1305 the king manipulated the election of a new French Pope, Clement V, who was elected in France because of the dire political uproar in Rome. Clement V did not return to Rome after his election, like some predecessors who had lived out of Rome. In 1309 he decided to live in Avignon, in the pleasant south of France.

It needs to be admitted that at this time Rome was a dangerous place to live for anyone, with warring families, such as the Orsini and Colonnas, controlling the area. For Popes it was a battle-ground and Clement felt it best to be out of it.

Clement V's move to Avignon would last for seven papal reigns over a period of 67 years. The Roman Curia also moved to Avignon. During this time the Pope and cardinals were acknowledged as secular princes and treated with royal dignity in the Pope's residence in Avignon. This Palais des Papes (Palace of the Popes) extended in size and grandeur and had all the trappings of royalty. The Popes lived under the protection of the French king. It was also considered right that the Papacy should now be run more like a temporal state.

The Papacy's administration and legislature reflected state models. It demanded taxes for the election of a bishop to a particular diocese; there was a tax on all church property; there was a fee for any dispensations from Church law. The Popes in Avignon thereby became very rich. Calls for the Papal Court to return to the poverty and simplicity of its supposed Christian origins were regarded as heretical.

Clement V saw three major problems before him: the Church's name had been lessened by the behaviour of the Papacy; the organisation of the Church required revitalisation; there were heretics, such as the Cathars, who were modern Gnostics, spreading in France and they needed, according to the mind of Clement and his successors, to be suppressed.

It is revealing to follow what happened at Avignon, Pope by Pope. There was no pattern observable. The succession after Clement V was as follows:

- Pope John XXII: 1316–1334. It took two years for the cardinals to decide on a successor to the first Avignon pope. John XXII was a compromise and was elected only after the secular powers demanded that something had to be done. Evidently he was a very ugly man, in ill health and not expected to live long. In fact he had a long reign during which he managed to bring about some reform in the administration of the Church.

- Pope Benedict XII: 1334–1342. Jacques Fournier, once an austere Cistercian monk, had earlier been the Inquisitor in charge of rooting out the heretical Cathars from their centres in the south. He was unexpectedly made Pope and chose to stay in Avignon. He built the sumptuous Palais des Papes to replace an earlier Papal residence, even though he continued to wear his Cistercian habit amid the luxury.

- Pope Clement VI: 1342–1352. He had been an advisor to the French king and was deemed well suited for the position of Pope. It was during his reign that the Great Plague exploded and wiped out a third of the European population. Despite this, he managed to live in great luxury in his Avignon Palace.
- Pope Innocent VI: 1352–1362. He was an old man when elected. He tried, despite his clearly French political leanings, to hold off any war between France and England. He was not successful.
- Pope Urban V: 1362–1370. He was regarded as a very holy man, but he was pressed by French demands and easily gave in.

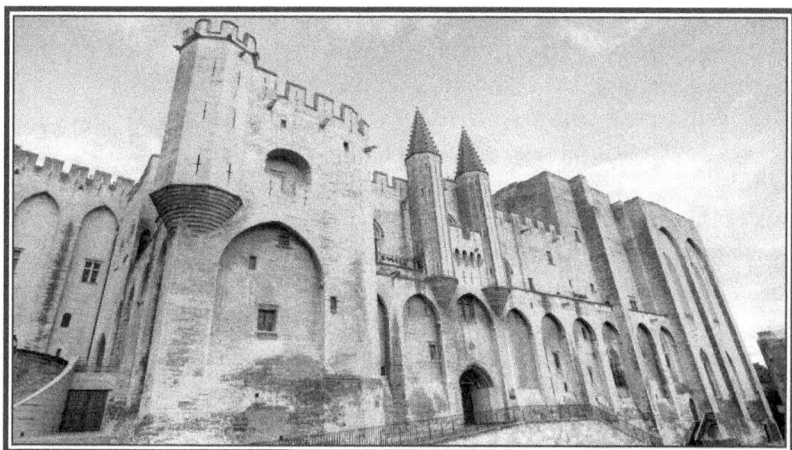

*Figure 11*
*The Palace of the Popes in Avignon*

The seventh Avignon pope was Gregory XI, historically of great importance, because it was his decision to return to Rome in September, 1376. Italy was in turmoil with groups of cities pitted against the Papacy mainly on economic grounds. The city of Florence for example had, for its uprising, been excommunicated by the Pope.

Catherine of Siena in central Italy, a mystic figure of great religious importance at that time, was demanding that the Pope return or there would be grave consequences. She addressed him with confidence: 'Ah, my dear Babbo (Daddy), see that you attend to these things!' Gregory did attend to her and did return. He died not long after. This period of the Popes in Avignon was later called 'The Babylonian Captivity of the Church', likened to the period of exile inflicted on the Jews after they had been forcibly deported from ruined Jerusalem by the Babylonians in 586 BCE.

## *The Great Schism*

✠ Urban VI (1378-1389)

✠ Boniface IX (1389-1404)

✠ Innocent VII (1404-06)

✠ Gregory XII (1406-15)

✠ Martin V (1417-31)

On Gregory XI's death in Rome, Urban VI (1378-1389) was elected, an Italian from Naples who made his dislike of the French very clear. During the Conclave the Roman crowd outside had demanded that only an Italian would be acceptable; they had had their fill of the French.

Very soon after the Conclave, the French cardinals withdrew from Rome and returned to Avignon, claiming to be unsafe in Rome. There, they went further and claimed that the Conclave had only elected Urban VI under physical duress, because of fear of the Italian mob. There are scholars who claim that this was indeed true and that the decision made under duress was made worse by the fact that those around Urban VI came to realise that he was violent and perhaps mentally deranged.

The French cardinals held another Conclave and elected their own Pope, Clement VII, who reigned from 1378-1394 in Avignon. There were now two Popes: a Roman one and a French one. Upon Clement VII's death he was succeeded by yet another Avignon Pope, Benedict XIII, who remained in place until 1423, although he was expelled from Avignon earlier.

This period, following on from the 'Babylonian Captivity of the Church', became known as the Great Schism or breakaway, when a substantial part of the Church was withdrawn from the authority of the Roman Pope. It would last from 1378-1417. During that time the people of Europe had little idea who the real Pope might be (given, as said above, that scholars have ever since been divided on the issue). France sided with the Avignon popes; England defended the Roman popes.

It was ludicrous. For some forty years the Papal courts at Avignon and Rome would have separate administrations, separate Conclaves and separate Popes. The Popes from each constituency issued papal decrees on various matters and appointed their own cardinals. The political leaders of the great powers of Europe played one Pope off against another to gain political advantages. The two Popes would sometimes side with now this nation and now another. The situation was intolerable for the Christian people.

To complete the Avignon story, after Benedict XIII there were three more Antipopes in Avignon although they had very little influence:

✠ Clement VIII (1423–1429)

✠ Benedict XIV (1424–1430).

> Elected in opposition to Clement VIII, who eventually abdicated.

✠ Benedict XIV (1430–1437)

Towards the end of the fiasco, there would be three Popes simultaneously, the third being elected at the Council of Pisa (which Church historians do not recognise as an Ecumenical Council).

This Council was held in the Cathedral of Pisa, next to the Leaning Tower, in 1409 by cardinals who were discontented with both the Avignon and the Roman contenders. They considered both to be ill-suited to the Papacy. As neither Pope appeared before the Council when requested, the Council deposed the Avignon Pope Benedict XIII and the Roman Pope Gregory XII, charging them with dividing the Church and with heresy. In their place the cardinals (fourteen from Avignon and ten from Rome) met and elected a new Pope, Alexander V. He reigned only for a year and had a successor John XXIII (1410-1415).[30]

The Council of Pisa had put forward a very contentious proposal in making their choice: they claimed that a meeting of bishops must be considered superior to the authority of any one bishop, even if that bishop was the Pope and Bishop of Rome.

Nothing changed. Except there were now three Popes!

Strident calls for reform were common after this, and the Emperor Sigismund, King of Germany and Hungary and eventually to be the Holy Roman Emperor, was constrained to call yet another Council at Constance, Germany, in 1414 CE. This convocation was approved by John XXIII, the reigning Pope in Pisa. At this Council, recognising that the issues were based largely on national differences, it was proposed that the voting should accordingly take place by national voting blocks, not individual votes. The Council lasted until 1418 and in 1417 it disposed of the three rival Popes. John XXIII, who saw the writing on the wall, tried to escape from Constance. He was arrested and brought back to the city where the Council deposed him. Gregory XII in Rome resigned[31] and the Avignon Pope, Benedict XIII, refusing to participate at the Council, was also deposed.

It then took two years to elect a new Pope, Martin V, who agreed to return to Rome.

The Council of Constance was held specifically to end the Three

Popes problem. However, it also raised the question from the Council of Pisa – Conciliarism. In 1415 the Council had passed a decree:

> Legitimately assembled in the Holy Spirit, constituting a general Council and representing the Catholic church militant, it has power immediately from Christ; and that everyone of whatever state or dignity, even Papal, is bound to obey it in those matters which pertain to the faith, the eradication of the said Schism and the general reform of the said Church of God in head and members.

However, the legitimacy of this decree has been rigorously rejected by the Catholic Church ever since. It is claimed that it was passed during the earlier part of the Council, when John XXIII was still in charge. He has been considered since as an Antipope (and this was presumed to be confirmed when Angelo Roncalli took his Papal name in 1958). Therefore the decree, it has been declared since, was invalid. Gregory XII, who reconvened the Council in its second year, before he resigned, had never affirmed the decree.

At least at this point, after so many tumultuous years, the Church had one single Pope, Martin V, and he was ruling in Rome. He found it dilapidated and poverty stricken. It was really a series of poor villages built amidst the ruins of earlier architectural finery.

*The Popes in Avignon had lost the goodwill of the European community generally. The French influence on Papal decisions, their nepotism (favouritism towards relatives and close friends in the bestowal of Church offices) and the taxes to uphold a lavish lifestyle were all well-known at the time. Further, the Cardinals had become like a Roman Senate attending its Emperor. They required the Pope to consult them.*

*Neither before nor since had the Papacy been on the brink of self-destruction as it had during the time of the Great Schism. The problem was not solved from within. It was only solved by the intervention of a Council. The Council deposed the three contending Popes; it was instrumental in having another Pope elected. Did this mean that the Pope was subject to a Council? Did it mean that a Council could intervene and elect a new Pope? To this day the possibilities inherent in this historical impasse are intriguing.*

*Certainly, the Avignon interlude shows to what extent the shape of the Papacy could and did change over time. It could hardly be compared to the 'Peter' elected by the early Christians in Rome.*

# *NOTES*

For a good general summary of Christian religion and its practice in the late Middle Ages see:

Swanson, R. (1995), *Religion and Devotion in Europe*, c. 1215-1515, CUP: Cambridge

On the Byzantine period and Byzantine Papacy, the Frankish Papacy, the Investiture Controversy, the East-West Schism, the Crusades and the Avignon Papacy see the following:

General texts:

Fossier, Robert and Sondheimer, Janet (1997). *The Cambridge Illustrated History of the Middle Ages*, CUP: Cambridge

Luscombe, David and Riley-Smith, Jonathan (2004), *New Cambridge Medieval History*: C.1024-c.1198. CUP: Cambridge

Mango, Cyril A. (2002). *The Oxford History of Byzantium*. Oxford: Oxford University Press

The Byzantines

Browning, R. rev. ed. (1980), *The Byzantine Empire*, Catholic University of America Press: Washington

Cameron, Averil (2006). *The Byzantines*. Oxford: Blackwell.

Gregory, Timothy E. (2010). *A History of Byzantium*. Malden: Wiley-Blackwell

The Crusades

Lock, Peter (2006). *Routledge Companion to the Crusades*. New York: Routledge

Tyerman, Christopher (2006). *God's War: A New History of the Crusades*. Cambridge, MA: Belknap Press.

# 7/
# THE POPES IN NEW TIMES

By the time some measure of stability had returned to the Papacy after the Avignon debacle, there was already the beginning of significant new political and cultural developments. Europe was going through its own cultural transformation. The markers for this transformation would be the Renaissance, the Reformation and the Enlightenment.

There was first the onset of a new cultural movement in Western Europe, called the Renaissance. The term means a 'rebirth', when people cultivated the study of the past, of classical times – particularly Roman and Greek art, architecture, thinking and literature – in order to appreciate their own culture to advantage.

The Popes generally would in time become patrons of the Renaissance arts and became immersed in the spirit of the age, bestowing money on projects (particularly the replacement of St Peter's Basilica with a new structure that would showcase the most prestigious architecture, art and sculpture and ensure that all could see the grandeur of the Papacy), and subsidising works of art and artists.

*Places like Rome became a focal point for the nurturing of this new vision of life.*

### The Renaissance Popes

✝ Eugene IV (1431-47)

✝ Nicholas V (1447-55)

✝ Callistus III (1455-58)

✝ Pius II (1458-64)

✝ Paul II (1464-71)

✝ Sixtus IV (1471-84)

✝ Innocent VIII (1484-92)

✝ Alexander VI (1492-1503)

✝ Pius III (1503)

✝ Julius II (1503-13)

✝ Leo X (1513-21)

✝ Adrian VI (1522-23)

✝ Clement VII (1523-34)

As the Popes had done in Avignon and earlier, the Renaissance Popes lived in luxury and promoted their families through the practice of nepotism. In Rome, 'cardinal-nephews' (blood relatives of the reigning Pope) became a standard and acceptable position in the Papal court and 'crown-cardinals' (relatives of the ruling powers in Europe or of the powerful Italian families) likewise. These actually were expected to become the leaders in the College of Cardinals and they could influence future elections.

As stated, Martin V had found a ruined Rome. Since that time, efforts were made to restore it as a suitable home for the Papacy. Although the Apostolic Palace on Vatican Hill had been built originally by Eugene III (1145-1153) and extended by later Popes, its real founder was Nicholas V (1447-1455), a humanist and someone interested in architecture. The Apostolic Palace as it stands today in Vatican City, however, was the later work of Sixtus V (1585-1590) and his successors. This has served as the home and working space of Popes and is part of what is referred to as 'The Vatican'.[32]

Papal Rome and the areas surrounding it had been maintained to this point largely by payments from spiritual benefits in the form of taxes, charges and donations. More, much more, was required. For one thing, in this period the Popes needed a standing army to defend their Papal States, from which a large part of their wealth derived. A Pope like Julius II (1503-1513), the so-called 'Warrior Pope', actually led his army into battle to defend and extend (on the basis of long-standing claims) his territories in the Papal States. It was said that he wore his Papal pectoral cross over his armour.

A major item of expenditure was the decision to rebuild St Peters. The old building was crumbling, beyond repair and disreputable. It needed to be replaced by something much more extensive and magnificent. There is a long tale of the demolition of the old St Peters, the planning for the new building and the vicissitudes of the building project from the time of Julius II onwards. In itself this story is enthralling, but the project would be enormously expensive.

*Figure 12 – Old St Peter's*

At the same time the Popes rarely cultivated Christian spirituality. They enjoyed a luxurious lifestyle; they had mistresses; they had children (Alexander VI had some eight children by three women). They dispensed monies freely from the Papal coffers for their personal purposes.

It was back to business for Papal absolutism and the problem of Conciliarism was duly forgotten.

In short the Popes of the Renaissance were indistinguishable from secular monarchs. They tried to intervene in world disputes; they arbitrated in conflicts between world powers. When both Portugal and Castile (in modern Spain) tried to take over colonial areas outside of Europe, it was the Pope (in this case Alexander VI) who organised which power could colonise and where.

However, the patronage of the arts and the new building program in Rome required finance, and the Church finances needed to be supplemented. By the time of the election of Leo X (1513-1521) the Papacy was utterly corrupt. On his election Leo stated: 'Let us enjoy the Papacy, since God has given it to us.' He was quite unable to tell that a revolution was brewing that would tear his disintegrating Church apart.

Leo was faced with a major question: how could the extravagance of church leaders, the financing of grandiose artistic plans and particularly the rebuilding of St Peter's be financed? In one blinding moment, an idea was conceived. From the Middle Ages there had been a church teaching that since Jesus, the Virgin Mary and the saints had earned huge extra merit before God, far more than they needed for themselves, this extra merit had been deposited in the 'Treasury of the Church' and the Pope had control of that Treasury.

Furthermore, the Church of the Middle Ages had seen the development of a belief in Purgatory, a state of terrifying punishment after death for those who had not completely alienated themselves from God, but who were not pure enough to be admitted immediately to heaven. We have seen that at first, remission of the time spent in purgatory, what was called an *indulgentia* or an 'indulgence', was promised to those Christian Crusaders who joined the Pope's armies and fought against the Muslim invaders of Palestine (particularly if they died in the endeavour); this indulgence was simply withdrawn by the Pope from the infinite Treasury of the Church.

The indulgence had persuaded the Crusaders. Why not extend the practice? The indulgence could be offered to those who did significant good works and they would be accorded a remission of the time to be spent in Purgatory; however, we saw that the common belief circulated that all sins of a lifetime could be remitted to a Crusader who died in battle. Leo X thought forward: instead of granting indulgences for good works such as participating in a Crusade, they could be granted to those who made a payment of money for the good of the Church. They could even be obtained for dead relatives, perhaps still languishing in Purgatory.

Most importantly, the indulgence could cover all sins. It was a brilliant solution and Leo X and his immediate successors made use of these payments to bolster the financial support for their favourite projects.

### The Popes of the Reformation

At this point a hitherto unknown Augustinian monk appeared, Martin Luther, professor of biblical studies at the University of Wittenberg. He challenged the corrupt practice of offering indulgences to Christians for money, as well as some other church teachings; there was, he rightly claimed, no basis for the practice in the Christian Scriptures or the earlier teaching of the Church. When challenged by the Church authorities, including Pope Leo X himself, he refused to give way. What had begun as a dispute over a sordid religious practice became a challenge to the highest authority in the Church.

*Figure 13*
*Martin Luther*

Attempts to bring about reconciliation failed. Luther was excommunicated by Leo X in 1520. The document of excommunication began: 'A wild boar has invaded Thy vineyard'. This Roman Bull was publicly burned by Luther with the words: 'This burning is only a trifle. It is necessary that the Pope and Papal See should also be burned. He who does not resist the Papacy with all his heart cannot obtain eternal salvation'.

Within Germany, Luther became the focal point of a reform movement that had been steadily developing for some time. In fact, the Pope and his teachings had been unwelcome there for generations. Luther's breakaway from the Roman Church, together with the formation of the Lutheran church and some others related to it, was the spark that ignited other reform movements throughout Europe. This was the start of the so-called Reformation.

In fact, the Reformation of the Roman Church gave rise to four main anti-Papal groups. There was first the Lutheran church that took its rise from Martin Luther and his rejection of the practice of indulgences and the pretentions of the Popes. Secondly, there was Calvinism, led by John Calvin, leading to the formation of Calvinism and, in Scotland, of Presbyterianism. John Calvin was much younger than Luther; the two never met. He left the Catholic Church around 1530 and was invited to reform the religious life of Geneva. It was there that he devised the principles of Calvinism.

Thirdly, there was the Anabaptist tradition which, around the same time as Luther, endeavoured to establish an ideal Christian community. Finally, there came the Anglican breakaway under Henry VIII. This breakaway had its own story.

While Western Europe was being divided in its religious loyalties, there had been unrest too in England. By the sixteenth century, Luther's writings and an English translation of the Bible, explicitly forbidden by Rome, were both being smuggled into the country from Europe. Henry VIII (1491-1547), the king of England from 1509, wanted no religious change and in 1521 he actually wrote a treatise against some of the teachings of Luther. For this he was given the title of 'Defender of the Faith' by the grateful Pope, the same Leo X who had excommunicated Luther.

However, Henry's real problem was not with Church teaching; it was more personal. He wanted to re-marry and he asked for the Pope to declare his first marriage invalid. Pope Clement VII refused. So, in 1534 Henry proclaimed himself Head of the Church in England and defied the authority of the Pope. This was the beginning of the Anglican Church. Henry was never a reformer in the real sense. In his thinking and even in his practice he remained true to the teaching of the Roman Church, apart from the fact that he would not accept the authority of the Pope. Real theological reform came about under his successors to the throne of England and their theologians.

These developing groups – the Lutherans, the Calvinists, the Anabaptists and the Anglicans – were linked as Protestants by their rejection of the authority of the Pope. Thus the Anglican Westminster Confession of 1646 states:

There is no other head of the Church but the Lord Jesus Christ: nor can the Pope of Rome in any sense be head thereof; but is that Antichrist, that man of sin and son of perdition, that exalts himself in the Church against Christ, and all that is called God. (24:6)

This is a clear rejection of the This-worldly Intermediary. What the Reformation revealed was the utter depravity and uselessness to which the Papacy had sunk for many Christians. Attracted by wealth, finery and power, the Popes had lost all sense of their ministry. They were merely playing out a fake religious role by which they could further their very worldly aims.

The Reformers would not accept this. Luther and others could see no mediation leading to Contact with Ultimacy in the existing Papacy. The Pope was not their This-worldly Intermediary. Nor were there any immediate indications that the Papacy would or even wanted to change. What eventuated for the Reformers was a structural change:

### Focus on Ultimacy: 'Abba/ Father

↓

### Other-worldly Intermediaries: the Divine Son of God, Jesus (plus the Spirit of God)

### (Contact Achieved)

### This-worldly Intermediary: the Literary Jesus (in the Bible)

↑

### Reformed Christian Church

The Reformers replaced the Pope with the text of The Bible, duly interpreted, reaching its climax in its presentation of the Literary Jesus. The shock of the Reformation had its own effect on the Papal institution.

The Papacy once again decided to reform.

☩ Paul III (1534-49)
☩ Julius III (1550-55)
☩ Marcellus II (1555)
☩ Paul IV (1555-59)

✝ Pius IV (1559-65)

✝ Pius V (1566-72)

✝ Gregory XIII (1572-85)

✝ Sixtus V (1585-90)

✝ Urban VII (1590)

✝ Gregory XIV (1590-91)

✝ Innocent IX (1591)

✝ Clement VIII (1592-1605)

✝ Leo XI (1605)

✝ Paul V (1605-21)

✝ Gregory XV (1621-23)

✝ Urban VIII (1623-44)

✝ Innocent X (1644-55)

While much of Europe and England were in religious turmoil and many rejected the Roman Church and the Papacy, the Roman Church did not remain unmoved. The reality of the breakaway of the Protestant churches finally roused the Papacy out of its downward slide and peaceful sloth. It undertook its own internal reform and this has become known as the Counter Reformation. Perhaps the term 'Counter Reformation' is unfair since some worthwhile reform had begun in the church even before the time of Luther's breakaway and some prefer the period to be called the 'Catholic Reformation'.

The Catholic Reformation officially began in 1534 when Pope Paul III called for a reform of 'Head and Members'. The fact that he included the Head, himself as the Pope, is interesting. As Alessandro Farnese he had been a typical Renaissance noble who, after being made a cardinal, still fathered four children. Then, he underwent a self-reform and around the time of Luther he began pressing for reform in the Church. Elected Pope he set up a reform commission to examine Church abuses. He also ensured that any new appointees to the College of Cardinals should be committed to reform. Under him the Jesuits, founded by Ignatius Loyola, were given the express purpose of being the loyal agents of the Pope, ready to carry out his bidding whenever and wherever he required.

But the most important step was to come. Under Paul III, another Ecumenical Council was called at Trent, in northern Italy. The Council was demanded by the Diet of Worms in 1521; this was a deliberative assembly of the Holy Roman Empire, held on this occasion in the city of

Worms. At the Diet, Luther had spoken and explained his theological challenges. In response, the Diet's text required a 'free, general Christian Council in German lands'. The wording was important. 'Free' meant that it was not under the sole authority of the Pope; it would be convened by the Emperor and the Pope together. 'Christian' referred to the fact that it would not be a solely clerical affair; laypeople would be involved. 'In German lands' referred to the location being within the Empire's boundaries and outside the Papal States.

This Council took some twenty-four years after the Diet of Worms to be convoked and the demands of the Diet were never fully met. It assembled for three sessions (1545-1547; 1551-1552; 1559-1563) in Trent, a delightful town situated in the north of Italy. The broad agenda for the Council was i) to heal the rift between the Protestants and the Church of Rome, ii) to reform the Church of Rome (the main issues being – political and financial corruption and bribery, sexual misbehaviour by the clergy, nepotism, the ignorance of many priests and the multiplicity of dioceses run by the same absentee bishop), and iii) to arrange for the defence of Europe in the face of the Ottoman Turks.

The Council considered many of the issues of belief and practice brought up by the Reformers themselves. However, against the request of the Reformers that the very structure of the medieval Church should change, the Council stood solid.

The Church with its hierarchy of Pope, bishops and priests would remain; likewise the sacramental system of seven rituals, identified by the Church as having been established by Jesus himself, was not open to discussion. However, the sale of indulgences for money was outlawed (although the practice of granting indulgences without monetary recompense continued). There were important measures taken to improve the education of the clergy. This had previously been left to individual circumstances, but no longer. Seminaries ('seedbeds') were set up for the systematic training of all future priests. Also, bishops were ordered to remain in their own diocese (and not act as absentee land-owners), to have only one diocese and to take pastoral care of their people.

However, on the broader questions of church teaching, Trent remained adamant. It considered the theological questions of the Reformers – God revealed himself by the Hebrew and Christian Scriptures only; Justification (the process by which Christian people found their salvation) is achieved by faith and not by good works; the priesthood belongs to the entire Church and not to an ordained male minority.

But Trent came out with its own conclusions: God had made his will known not only in Scripture but also through Tradition (the later teaching of the Church and particularly teaching sanctioned by the Pope); justification was by both faith and good works; there was a separate ordained clergy, who alone could administer the main sacraments, and these stood above the non-ordained believers. On so many matters, whereas the reformers wanted 'either-or', the Council of Trent decided on 'both-and'.

What resulted from Trent was a somewhat reformed Roman Catholic Church that was pitted against the breakaway reform groups in Europe and England. What had been decided at Trent would affect the Roman Church until the twentieth century.

Towards the end of the Council of Trent, the Pope was Paul IV (1559-1561), who had been Cardinal Gian Pietro Caraffa. He had been a staunch reformer since the time of Luther and had been made cardinal by Paul III because of his reforming spirit. However, he was very different to Paul III. The latter was a cultured gentleman, who hoped to reform the Church within the limits of creativity offered by the Renaissance. Paul IV's idea of reform was conservatism. He set out as Pope to construct with vigour a new style of Church. His reform measures intended to extirpate all heresy within the Roman Church. He did this by first establishing the Index of Prohibited books. Only those books considered by the Papal authorities as fit to be read could be made available to Catholics. Then there was a revival of the Inquisition, a practice that had been used in the past for particular manifestations of heresy and in which Paul IV, as a cardinal, had been involved. The Inquisition was a travelling ecclesiastical court that examined charges of heresy and had the power to inflict even the death penalty. Paul IV commented that 'were even my father a heretic, I would gather the wood to burn him'. The Inquisition took its most severe form in Spain where not only suspect Christians but converted Jews were examined with rigour and with some executions (although not as many died as legend has it).

Most importantly, Paul IV saw no purpose in further negotiating with the heretical Protestants.

These rigorous practices tended to subdue personal religious sentiment in the Roman Church. In its place the new-look Church turned to absolute obedience to clerical superiors and written law and regulations, regular observance of the Mass (which had been standardised in prayer and action almost everywhere by Trent) and the other sacraments, the performance of penances, such as fasting during Lent and other special occasions, and the careful recital of rote prayers such as the Rosary.

It was under a later successor of Paul IV, Sixtus V (1585-1590), that this reformed Church was re-presented to the world as a pure and attractive thing. He himself was of upper class birth and came from a wealthy family. He was well educated and cared for by his Church patrons.

The Baroque Age in art was dawning, the time when the arts indulged in exaggerated detail. It was also the time for the dramatic style in all cultural display; in architecture for example, the palaces made use of grand staircases (of which one of the best examples is the Scala Regia, the flowing staircase in the Apostolic Palace) and opulent reception rooms. Sixtus, while upholding the decrees of Trent, promoted the Church in Rome as something at the forefront of the Baroque revival. He spent lavishly on Baroque art. He had the Sistine Chapel (named after him) adjacent to St Peter's built and decorated in a magnificent painting style. Importantly, within this Sistine Chapel he commissioned from Michelangelo two matched fresco cycles of the life of Moses and the life of Jesus. 'Moses', as all were presumed to know, was the symbol of a ruling Pope. The city of Rome was about to become a symbol of Papal greatness, with a reorganised city and a reorganised Papal Curia. The groundwork was laid for the Catholic Church as it was to remain up to the 1960s.

In 1620 a Catholic army, made up of international troops, defeated the Protestants, who had followed Fredrick of Bohemia, near Prague. This was the end of the Protestant attempt to take central Europe by force. It seemed that this would mean success for the political Catholic intervention that had been in vogue since the end of the Council of Trent. But the Thirty Years War ended in 1648 without the triumph of a Catholic Europe. There were too many vested interests for the victors to go with either Catholic or Protestant. The Peace of Westphalia, a treaty which deliberately went against Papal policy, was condemned by Innocent X with a Bull that set out to 'condemn, reprove, quash and annul' the treaty.

From the time of this Innocent X (1644-1655), the inability for the Papacy to see what was happening in Europe was manifest. When eyes were scrutinising the Vatican, Pope Innocent blithely ruled in grand style with the assistance of his dead brother's widow, Donna Olimpia Maidalchini-Pamphili. The relationship may not have been sexual, but she dominated the whole of the Papal court and made it a laughing-stock. Papal decisions were not made without her consent; she proposed those who were to be promoted in the Curia and other offices. Only Innocent's death brought this uncomfortable liaison to a conclusion.

The episode was typical of the times.

*It seemed that there had been progress in the reformation of the Church of Rome, led by reforming Popes. Clergy were being educated in a systematic way; bishops were being appointed so that they could care for a single diocese. There were lapses in both areas, but nothing like the earlier times when clergy were ignorant and bishops were feudal lords.*

*Religious devotions among Roman Catholics, based on endless rote prayers, on devotion for scandalous relics of deceased saints (many spurious) and even angels (all spurious), on admiration for abnormal religious experiences were being purified of their excesses. Worship in the Roman Church became more dignified and regulated, and enabled the common people to find religious contact. The Church had refined more and more its attitude to Missions in foreign lands, seeing them no longer as a means of colonisation and the acquisition of personal wealth; there was more respect and genuine care for indigenous peoples.*

*In this atmosphere, the theologian Roberto Bellarmino (1542-1621) redefined the Papacy. Like the absolute rulers of France, England and Spain, the Papacy was an absolute monarchy established by God, he wrote. The Head of this Church is still Jesus Christ. The Pope is his visible Vicar. If a Council passes any decrees, they require the Pope's approval to become law. The Pope cannot be judged by any other, cannot be deposed or punished by any other, including a General Council. The Pope requires an efficient bureaucracy but is not dependent on it. The Church revolves around the Pope. This statement together with a seemingly reformed Papacy became the popular image until the present time.*

*The new prestige of a reforming Papacy only stirred up Protestant hostility. Protestants searched the Book of Daniel and the Book of Revelation and claimed that the Catholic Church and the Pope were depicted in both. The Pope was The Anti-Christ and the Church was the Synagogue of Satan.*

*Yet for the Roman Church it seemed that a new dawn was about to break. Perhaps the Reformers would return to the fold when they saw the reformed Church and a reformed Papacy.*

*It was not to be.*

## *The Popes of the Enlightenment*

Western Europe had been split asunder in its religious allegiances between the Roman Church and the Reformers. The monopoly on power of the Roman Church, which had continued despite the most dreadful lapses of the Popes, was over. But the formation of Reform Churches at odds with the Church of Rome and the Popes together with the reaction of the Catholic Reformation was not the end of turmoil in Europe.

From about the middle of the seventeenth century, Europe would be convulsed by a new intellectual movement, called The Enlightenment, which targeted both the Roman Church and the Reformers. It would last throughout the eighteenth century. Its goal was to reform the whole of society from the ground up. Its main enemy was the irrationality of religion which prescribed unacceptable beliefs and an inauthentic ethical way of life, to be accepted without question, on the basis of ancient texts from the Bible and decrees from the Popes. The Enlightenment wanted Reason to replace Religious Tradition. It was also determined to remove widespread superstition (regarding images, regarding relics, regarding religious rituals) that had become protected by religion and to counter the religious tyranny that had seen protestors and forward thinkers silenced and executed.

The Enlightenment had been given a voice by a series of great philosophers. Among the more prominent were Voltaire (a pen-name for François-Marie Arouet) and Denis Diderot. The latter undertook the production of a mammoth *Encyclopédie* to which the greatest thinkers of the age contributed. The issues became clearer as the text of the *Encyclopédie* spread from country to country.

There was first the demand that all thinking be based solely on Reason. It was not to be based on the Church's reading of the Bible or on Church tradition handed on unquestioningly from ancient times. The Enlightenment heralded the birth of the scientific method and science quickly disassociated itself from religion, whether that of the Church or that of the Reformers. Many of the philosophers took up Deism, a belief in an uninvolved God who set the cosmos in motion but then withdrew and allowed it to take its own course. Voltaire called this God 'The Great Watchmaker'.

All Religion found it necessary to respond to the challenge. The Popes became involved in different ways in The Enlightenment debate.

✝ Alexander VII (1655-67)
✝ Clement IX (1667-69)
✝ Clement X (1670-76)
✝ Innocent XI (1676-89)
✝ Alexander VIII (1689-91)
✝ Innocent XII (1691-1700)
✝ Clement XI (1700-21)
✝ Innocent XIII (1721-24)
✝ Benedict XIII (1724-30)
✝ Clement XII (1730-40)
✝ Benedict XIV (1740-58)
✝ Clement XIII (1758-69)
✝ Clement XIV (1769-74)
✝ Pius VI (1775-99)
✝ Pius VII (1800-23)

As the Enlightenment thinkers encroached more and more on what the Roman Church saw as its domain, the Church became defensive. It upheld the value of the Bible, it even in desperation decided to show more toleration towards the Protestants. But the Enlightenment would mean the serious decline of Papal prestige and Papal power in Europe.

There is a story, possibly apocryphal, that on his death bed Voltaire, one of the Encyclopedists, was asked by a priest to renounce Satan. He replied: 'Now, now, my good man, this is no time for making enemies.' This parody sums up the Enlightenment attitude to the Church at the time.

Even after Innocent X, the Popes were more interested in other things – particularly the finances and protection of the Papal States. Accordingly, they became involved in European politics and tried to manipulate one state against another state for their own advantage. At a time when the Church floundered and did not know where it was going, one after another aged and incompetent Pope would be elected as a compromise, as cardinals found themselves unable to agree on a suitable successor.

An exception was Prospero Lambertini who became Benedict XIV (1740-1758). He had been involved in the arts and culture before his accession to the Papacy. Subsequently, as Pope, he dabbled in Enlightenment thought and promoted experimental science, particularly medical science. He even saw a future for women in the academic and scientific world – most unusual for the time. He was probably the only example of a true

Enlightenment Pope, one who could accept the intellectual premises of the day and debate with the scholars of the day on their own terms. He was however very much the exception.

The Jesuits had become involved too in European politics. As stated earlier, they were supposed to be the protectors of the Papacy. There were persistent calls for their suppression, particularly from the rulers of France and Spain. So pressing was the matter that when Clement XIV (1769-1774) was elected it was only on the proviso, promised to the Conclave beforehand, that he would dissolve the Order. He carried out his mandate and they were dispersed, not to be reinstated until 1814.

Then, as the Enlightenment went unchecked, arousing more and more unrest in Europe, the American Revolution broke out in 1775. Its roots were in the Enlightenment and its principles. Much closer to Europe there was, soon after, the French Revolution, one of whose triggers had been the American Revolution. It convulsed France, the Church's 'eldest daughter', in 1789. Almost in an instant, France seceded from the Papacy. A new French constitution made the Catholic religion a state affair; bishops and priests would be henceforward appointed by civilian officials. Rome and the Pope were to have no further say in the activity of the French church.

These decisions strengthened the opposition of the Papacy towards the revolutionaries. Liberty, equality and fraternity were seen as the enemies of the Church. It would take until the twentieth century for the Papacy to come to terms with the modern world.

Giovanni Angelo Braschi had been elected as Pius VI (1779-1799) during this revolutionary time and he condemned the new French constitution in 1791. But the old order in Europe had collapsed and the Papacy had no longer any protection from foreign powers; the Pope's appeals would not be heeded. Some years later, Italy was invaded by French troops and Pius VI was forced into exile where he would die in 1799 in France. The local French clergy refused to bury him and his death was registered as: 'Citizen Braschi, exercising the profession of Pontiff'.

Many thought that this was the end of the Papacy. There would not be another Pope. But Pius VI had the last laugh. Before he died he secretly arranged for a Conclave to meet in Venice and elect his successor.

The rift between the Roman Church and France was not solved until this Conclave was held in 1800. Pius VII (1800-1823) was elected. He managed within a year to establish a Concordat of Agreement with

Napoleon and the French government. But the harmony would not last. At Napoleon's coronation the Pope was allowed to anoint Napoleon and bless his crown, but the Emperor crowned himself. Eventually Pius VII, like his predecessor, was forced out of Rome by Napoleon. After the fall of Napoleon in 1815 at Waterloo, the Pope returned in triumph to Rome and was acclaimed by the populace. Interestingly, Pius VII beseeched the English not to be cruel to the captive Napoleon, and he himself safely harboured senior members of the Emperor's family in Rome.

*The Enlightenment thought-world had provided a framework for the Revolutions of the eighteenth century, for the rise of capitalism in Europe and for the proposal to establish socialism as the philosophical basis of European society. It was certainly not a thought-world and a social world that was aligned to the thinking of the Church or even aligned to the Reformed Churches. The subsequent Popes would have to cope with all this.*

*Whereas once they had controlled and directed the thinking of the populace, they now found themselves at odds with it.*

### The Popes after the Enlightenment

The Congress of Vienna in 1815 restored most of the Papal States to the Vatican. The fact that the Pope was firmly entrenched as a secular ruler seemed necessary for European peace. Napoleon had shown what would happen to the Papacy if it was not protected by secular rule: the spiritual power would be subordinated to secular forces.

✞ Leo XII (1823-29)
✞ Pius VIII (1829-30)
✞ Gregory XVI (1831-46)
✞ Pius IX (1846-78)
✞ Leo XIII (1878-1903)

The Popes who now followed in this new world, where Church was set against State and where Church thinking was inimical to popular thinking, were led by Leo XII (1823-1829). He was supported in the Conclave that elected him by a conservative group who saw in him the hope that the Church would return to its spiritual roots. He tried desperately to gain the upper hand. He enacted decrees against liberalism, indifferentism (the teaching that all religions are valid and it is a matter of a person's choice between them) and Freemasonry. He established a police regime in the Papal States, he restricted the Jews to their Roman Ghetto (with 300 of them being required to attend a Christian sermon every week) and even tried to rid the Vatican of unbecoming art and sculpture (all nudity in Vatican art and sculpture being clumsily covered over with plaster fig-leaves). He did not win over the populace. Indeed, the Roman people rejoiced when he passed away in 1829.

Another enemy of the new ways was Gregory XVI (1831-1846). Earlier he had written a book, *Il Trionfo della Santa Sede contro gli Assalti dei Novatori* ('The Triumph of the Holy See against the Attacks of the Innovators'). It summed up the Papacy at the time: the Popes were at war with society. Of importance, his book promoted the notion of Papal Infallibility, the theological idea that the Pope's formal teaching on faith and morals is always guaranteed to be free from error. The Infallibility of the Pope had been first voiced among scholars during the Middle Ages, but it only became a substantial part of Church thinking during the Catholic Reformation. More and more it was now surfacing and Gregory had given it a Papal voice.

On becoming Pope, Gregory XVI was faced with an insurrection in the Papal States. His subjects complained that there was systemic corruption in government and a blindness to the needs of the people. When he died the papal hold on the Papal States was becoming very tenuous. There was more interest being shown in forming a secular Italian political unity, encompassing the whole of the Italian peninsular, and that meant ousting Papal civil rule.

By this stage, the Church had adopted ever more a siege mentality. As they looked back, it was convinced that the American Revolution of 1776, the French Revolution of 1789 and particularly the movement towards Italian unity were all spawned by the ideas of the Enlightenment, and the Church was opposed to all of these revolutionary movements. It would refuse to accept the new thinking that underlay them and would defend itself against it. Into this negative ethos came Pius IX (1846-1978). He has been known universally by his Italian name, Pio Nono. He still holds the record for the longest Papal reign, one of just over thirty-one years.[33]

Pius IX, regarded by historians as a most autocratic Pope, showed his intransigent opposition to any of the new strains of Enlightenment thought. He was struggling to maintain his authority as Pope and political control of the Papal States. In 1848 he had to flee Rome (disguised as a parish priest) as republican forces took over Rome. He returned in 1850 but was then convinced that democracy had to be restrained. Within the Church, but outside Rome, there were even those who no longer saw the need for a Pope.

*Figure 14*
*Pio Nono (Pius IX)*

In 1864 he issued a document entitled *The Syllabus of Errors*. In it he condemned propositions which would seem perfectly reasonable today. Some examples of the *unacceptable* propositions are:

15. Everyone is free to embrace and profess that religion which is considered to be true according to human reason.

17. There is at least a good hope that all those who do not belong to the true church of Christ (i.e. the Catholic Church) will find their eternal salvation.

77. Today it is no longer proper that the Catholic religion should be regarded as the sole religion of the state, to the exclusion of all other forms of worship.

78. In some Catholic countries, wise legislation has decreed that people coming to reside therein shall enjoy the public exercise of their own peculiar worship.

79. The Roman Pontiff can and should reconcile himself, and come to terms with progress, liberalism and modern civilisation.

The *Syllabus*, as can be seen in these examples, was a strident claim that there should be no freedom of conscience, no freedom of the press, no free parliamentary systems, no equality before the law. This was the reaction of the nineteenth century Papacy, and particularly of Pius IX, to what was then modern thinking and the modern worldview.

It needs to be said that the *Syllabus* has to be read in context. Pope Pius IX firmly believed that the Catholic Church was the perfect society, that it had the complete and exclusive grasp of all truth, that it contained in itself all the resources required to achieve its own spiritual goal. In that context, it made some sort of sense. But, there was more to come. After the publication of the *Syllabus*, Pius IX convoked a council, Vatican I, which met in 1870.

As might be expected in a period of grave crisis, Vatican I passed decrees that declared that the Pope had supreme authority in the Church and was indeed infallible. This had been the ultimate aim of the Ultramontanes ('beyond the mountains', stating that the Pope's power spreads beyond the Alps), who held to the absolutism of the Papacy, the Pope's universal authority over faith and morals and the centralisation of the Church of Rome. Some of these Ultramontanes had hoped for a decree that would go further and state the Pope to be infallible in all his teaching, not just in his teaching on faith and morality. Such a decree would bolster his spiritual power just when he was being stripped of temporal power by the removal of his Papal States. Even so, the Pope emerged from Vatican I with a monopoly on ecclesiastical authority.

Berating a Cardinal at Vatican I who claimed that all bishops are witnesses to the Church's tradition, *Pio Nono* had replied to him: 'I am the Tradition'. This was arrogance not seen before. No previous Pope had claimed to have a direct hotline to God. The final decree on Infallibility was hedged around with conditions: the Pope had to make it clear he was speaking as Head of the Church and he had to be dealing with faith and morals and he had to make it clear that he was invoking his infallibility.

Hence, *Pio Nono* claimed infallible authority and he saw himself as delegating a share of his authority to bishops and they, in turn, delegated it to their priests. Lay people were the unnamed ones. Worship, teaching and Church government were completely in the hands of the clerical hierarchy under the direction of the Pope. This might have made sense in the earlier pre-modern worldview, where the world was a finished product of unchanging essences, with an inbuilt order directed to a fixed purpose. However, having an infallible Pope no longer made sense in the nineteenth century.

On the other side, spurred on by Enlightenment ideals, scholars had turned to the study of society and the study of humanity. Charles Darwin's

*Origin of Species* caused a rethinking of the whole history of humanity. History in general was re-thought and the scientific method was applied to the way in which sources were interrogated. Society and its structures were examined scientifically by sociologists. In these fields, if there was a case for evolution and for a changing and fluid view of what made up nature and society, then where did this leave the Bible which taught of creation and a fixed society? The Bible seemed to have taught humankind these things for millennia. The Church would need to defend the Bible.

It must be realised that the Catholic Church had not been really engaged in anything like a real study of the Bible. The Reformers had insisted on the Bible as the source of their teaching. Catholics had insisted on Tradition, the teaching authority of the popes and the bishops and the sacramental system as well as the Bible. But the Bible was only used by Catholics as a means of proving traditional doctrines and substantiating established practices, providing a 'mine' from which proof-texts might be extracted to prove what were already long-standing Church teachings and practices. A study of the Bible would not change anything. For this reason the Bible had been kept in its Latin translation; it was only required by the ordained ministers.

At the same time as meeting these intellectual challenges, Pius IX was caught up in a virtual maelstrom of historical events. Rome was not at that time the capital of the Italian provinces; the capital had been Florence since 1865. There was a concerted movement to unite Italy and to form a secular government. The new Italian government's armies defeated the Papal States in 1870 and then advanced on Rome itself. This marked the end of deliberation at Vatican I. It was never formally concluded.

The first Italian king, Victor Emmanuel, took over the Quirinal Palace in Rome, once a papal possession and home to some past Popes, and Rome became once again the capital of Italy. The Pope's territories were confined now to the Vatican, the area attached to Saint Peter's and the Apostolic Palace. During the last eight years of his reign Pius IX was forced to remain within the Vatican, never leaving its confines. Amongst Catholics world-wide the 'Prisoner of the Vatican' description of him became a sore point. In retaliation against the new Italian state, Pius forbade Italian Catholics to take place in any national elections in Italy, either by voting or being a candidate. They could only vote in local elections.

Pius IX died in 1878, embittered by the opposition, intellectual and political, that surrounded him. He was succeeded by Giocchino Pecci who took the name of Leo XIII (1878-1903), a very learned and cultured person; however, he was already an old man at his election and somewhat reclusive. As so often happened, he lived much longer than any of the Papal electors expected. He continued the path of the former Pope and decried the formation of an anti-Catholic Italy (in 1881 a furious Roman mob attempted to throw the coffin, bearing the corpse of Pius IX to its final resting place, into the Tiber). He intervened with vigour when he saw the new Italian State overstepping the boundaries: taking over Catholic churches and property, promoting a secular education policy. He considered moving to another city, such as Salzburg or Trieste, where he might gain Austrian protection. That did not come to pass.

His interests and influence, despite the dire problems in Rome, were wide. He had been a diplomat and he improved relations between the sealed-off Vatican and a number of European governments. He became involved in the struggle for workers' rights and social justice throughout the world. His encyclical letter on social justice, *Rerum Novarum*, is still cited by some writers for upholding workers' rights and particularly their right to form unions.[34] Leo XIII's influence in the social area was long-lived.

He also realised, as Pius IX had not, that the study of the Bible was vital if any credibility might be retained for the teaching of the Church. He saw that what the Councils of Trent and Vatican I had stated was completely inadequate in this regard. He took the bull by the horns and wrote an Encyclical on the study of the Bible in 1893 that shocked many in the Church. It was called *Providentissimus Deus*.

In fact, biblical scholars of the Catholic Church at this stage were in disarray, not knowing which direction to take. In an endeavour to provide such direction, Leo XIII's Encyclical showed an awareness of what was happening in the world of biblical scholarship and cautiously allowed Catholic scholars to investigate the Bible as literature. Yet, it also revealed some fear and restraint regarding new developments. He wrote:

> There has arisen, to the great detriment of religion, an inept method, dignified by the name of the 'higher criticism'[35], which pretends to judge the origin, the integrity and authority of each book from internal indications alone...It will not throw on the Scripture the light which is sought, or prove of any advantage to doctrine... seeing that most of them (the biblical critics) are tainted with false philosophy and rationalism, it must lead to the elimination from the sacred

writings of all prophecy and miracles, and of everything else that is outside the natural order.

This referred to the more recent study of the Bible, almost exclusively among scholars within the Reformed Churches, which found a series of underlying documents or traditions in the Hebrew Scriptures together with evidence of editing. For example, scholars found that the first five books of the Bible, the Pentateuch, had been written using earlier documents. They claimed that the Prophecy of Isaiah was really composed of three documents, from quite different periods, edited into one. In the study of the Christian Scriptures there was agreement that, prior to the four gospels, there had been a time when oral traditions circulated and that there had been earlier collections of Jesus materials. The four gospels had made use of a variety of such sources and contained discrepancies that could not be reconciled. As might be expected, Leo cautioned Catholic scholars about such conclusions.

Although it sounds so strange today, he also made it clear that the interpretation of Scripture should be a wholly Catholic affair:

> For although the studies of non-Catholics, used with prudence may sometimes be of use to the Catholic student, he should, nevertheless, bear in mind – as the Fathers also teach in numerous passages – that the sense of Holy Scripture can nowhere be found incorrupt outside the Church, and cannot be expected to be found in writers who, being without the true faith, only gnaw the bark of the sacred Scripture and never attain its pith.

This fear gave rise to something quite unfortunate. Around the turn of the century the heresy of Modernism was born, or perhaps it should be said it was invented. It was the most elusive of all Church heresies, a catch-all term constructed in the mind of the Church authorities to cover all those challenges that dismayed them. The heresy's biblical representative was a remarkable man, Alfred Loisy (1857-1940), a French priest and a professor of biblical studies.

Loisy had studied the liberal, Protestant 'Higher Criticism' (to which Leo XIII referred above) and had made use of some of its methods in his own doctoral research. However, in reaction to those critics who maintained that the institutional and visible Church was superfluous, that only an interior and personal Christian response was required for salvation, Loisy upheld the Catholic Church as the true Intermediary between God and humanity, even if he denied that the historical Jesus had actually founded it. His famous dictum was that 'Jesus proclaimed the coming of the Kingdom, but what came was the Church'. He accepted the then popular distinction between the Jesus of History (a Jesus who could be described purely on historical grounds) and the Christ of Faith (what the Scriptures and Tradition had made of the historical Jesus) and submitted that the early Christian community, with its particular theological bias, was an impenetrable barrier standing between the believer and the historical Jesus. Many Catholic biblical scholars would today agree with him.

Loisy and other so-called Modernists, people motivated by honesty and scholarship, were treated with some understanding by Leo XIII, who died in 1903, but the incoming pope, Pius X (1903-1914), would be someone very different.

*The eighteenth and nineteenth centuries showed the inability of the Papacy to deal with the changing culture of the times. It had reformed internally to a large extent but it was not able to confront the reality of new times. Pius IX had shown that the Church was adrift in the modern world. Leo XIII had attempted to force a way back, but it was very slow and he was getting older. By the end of the nineteenth century it has to be said that the Papacy claimed much, but was not able to deliver.*

# *NOTES*

Most general histories of the Renaissance and Reformation will include a study of the Popes of the period. Here are some relevant texts:

Cameron, E. sec. ed. (2012), *The European Reformation*, Oxford University Press: Oxford

Estep, W. (1986), *Renaissance & Reformation*. Eerdmans: Grand Rapids

Hale, J. ed. (1981), *The Thames and Hudson Encyclopaedia of the Italian Renaissance*, Thames and Hudson, London

Stinger, Charles L. (1998), *The Renaissance in Rome*. Indiana University Press: Bloomington

Thomsett, M. (2011), *Heresy in the Roman Catholic Church: a history*. McFarland: Jefferson, N.C.

The Enlightenment is usually treated in terms of philosophers and their ideas. The Popes only come in incidentally.

Fitzpatrick, M. et al., eds. (2004), *The Enlightenment World*, Routledge: London

Yolton, J. et al. (1992), *The Blackwell Companion to the Enlightenment*, Blackwell: Oxford

For the nineteenth-century Popes see:

Chadwick, O. (1998), *History of the Popes 1830-1914*, OUP: Oxford

Chiron, Yves (2005), *Pope Pius IX: The Man and the Myth*, Angelus Press: Kansas City

Hasler, August Bernhard (1981). *How the Pope Became Infallible: Pius IX and the Politics of Persuasion*. Doubleday: Garden City.

Hasler's book suggests that Pio Nono had an illegitimate son (conceived before he was ordained a priest, but while he was studying for the priesthood), Filippo Maria Guidi. Certainly there was a Guidi who became a Dominican priest. He quickly rose up the ranks and was made Archbishop of Bologna by Pio Nono, when that area was under foreign control and a clever diplomat was required. He was never able to take over his new diocese. Later, Guidi was made a Cardinal by Pio Nono when he was about 50.

As Cardinal Guidi, he attended Vatican 1 from 1879 and was very hesitant about the declaration on Infallibility. He spoke in the Assembly and wanted changes made to the formulation about it, restricting its possible usage. Pio Nono publicly upbraided him. Some of the Fathers at the Council laughed about what they saw as a father-son stand-off.

Whether the Guidi story of being Pio Nono's son is true or not (and it could be a tale), there is another strange but more substantiated story about this Pope. Edgardo Mortara was a Jewish child in Bologna who was secretly baptised by a Catholic servant who feared that he was dying and would not go to Heaven. Because he was a Christian now and no longer a Jew, Pio Nono stood against popular opinion and arranged for the boy to be kidnapped from his Jewish parents and brought to Rome. Eventually he was adopted by Pio Nono. At 21 the boy was ordained a priest and was awarded a stipend from Pio Nono for the rest of his life.

For further detail see:

Kertzer, D. (1997), *The Kidnapping of Edgardo Mortara*, Picador: London.

Another interesting fact was that Pio Nono was an epileptic. He was only ordained on condition that another priest attend him every time he said Mass in case he had a fit. This was later rescinded when his epileptic fits lessened in frequency. However, this medical fact must be taken into account when Pio Nono claimed to have had a vision of the Virgin Mary.

# 8/
# THE MODERN POPES

By the end of the nineteenth century the Papacy was at an all-time low in world prestige. Anthropology, history, geology, sociology were all throwing up problems that challenged the Church and challenged the Papacy.

It was Leo XIII who, to some extent, turned things around and faced the twentieth century with far less of a siege-mentality than his immediate predecessors. He had dealt with the world of labour and economics and he had seen the need to face the new developments in the study of the Bible and the expression of theological thinking.

These tentative steps forward by Leo XIII were to be reversed by Giuseppe Sarto as Pius X (1903-1914).

☦ Pius X (1903-14)
☦ Benedict XV (1914-22)
☦ Pius XI (1922-39)
☦ Pius XII (1939-58)

## *Pius X*

Pius X had been a pious and zealous country priest, with no pretensions to academic ability and little interest in scholarly matters, who advanced, despite his own protestations, through the ecclesiastical ranks to become the Patriarch of Venice. From there he was elected to the Papacy on the death of Leo XIII.

His experience had been confined to the culture of Italian social and family structures. Then as Pope he was confronted with Loisy and other 'Modernists', and he panicked. He did not understand, and perhaps could not understand, that there was a new world on his doorstep. There was no choice in his mind between protecting his faithful, ignorant, Catholic flock and dallying with some new biblical or theological theory. The theory would have to go.

In 1903, the year of Leo's death, Loisy had published a splendid book summarising his ideas on Jesus and the early church, *L'Évangile et l'Église* ('The Gospel and the Church'). Pius X immediately placed it on the Church's Index of Prohibited Books. Pius' own biblical method can be seen from an Encyclical which he published in the following year to commemorate the fiftieth anniversary of the Catholic Church's declaration that Mary had been immaculately conceived. It betrays the literalistic and simplistic Biblical interpretation of the pre-modern era.

> Adam wept in his punishment but he perceived Mary crushing the serpent's head. Noah in the safety of the Ark looked forward to her. So did Abraham as his hand was stayed. Likewise Jacob when he saw a ladder standing on the earth, with its top reaching up into heaven; a stairway for the angels of God to go up and come down. Moses saw her in the bush that was alight and did not burn. David sang of her as he danced before the Ark of the Covenant. Elias saw her in the little cloud rising up out of the sea. But why go on?

Indeed Loisy, reading such fundamentalist nonsense, must have wondered – why go on? Nevertheless, he sent a conciliatory letter to Pius X. It was never answered. Instead, Pius sent a message to the Archbishop of Paris ordering Loisy 'to burn what he adored and adore what he had burned'. Loisy recognised that he could not continue within the Catholic Church.

In 1908 he was excommunicated. In what might be interpreted as a vindictive action Pius declared him *vitandus*, he was to be physically avoided by all Catholics. He left his professorship and the Church with great sorrow and bitterness and took up a university posting. Only years after his death would his considerable contribution to biblical studies be even unofficially recognised by scholars within the Catholic church.

It has to be said that Pius X virtually crushed a generation of budding Catholic theological and biblical scholars. With his approval, a network of ecclesiastical espionage units, under an organisation called *Sodalitium Pianum* (the Sodality of Pius V), reported to Rome on deviant priests who preached or taught anything that seemed to be in any way unorthodox.

It was a dark era for Catholic scholarship in general, and biblical scholars were badly treated.

The Biblical Commission, set up by Leo XIII to give some arbitration between biblical scholars and the authority of the Church, became more menacing under Pius X, issuing a series of very fundamentalist decrees. It stated that Moses was the sole author of the Pentateuch and that the first three chapters of Genesis, which told of the creation of the world and the story of Adam and Eve, were to be understood in a literal and historical sense. It decreed that there was insufficient evidence to warrant the prophecy of Isaiah being assigned to three authors. In dealing with the Christian Scriptures it decided that Matthew had been the first gospel (which very few scholars ever accepted), written in Hebrew or Aramaic and then translated into Greek without any perceptible change. The authorship of the Gospel of John was attributed to the John who was one of The Twelve, and he was, the Commission stated, an eyewitness to the events he narrated. On all these points the Commission took up a stance starkly at odds with the findings of biblical scholars at that time.

The reign of Pius X established a pattern of repression of Church scholarship and a repression of attempts to connect the Church with developing cultures. The Church bureaucracy felt that it must control theological thinking and the interpretation of the sources of scholarship, and there was an authoritarian hold on morality. There was little attempt to reverse this trend until Vatican II.

Yet, it too would fail in the end.

### Benedict XV

Just as World War I broke out, Pius X died and was replaced by Giacamo della Chiesa, Benedict XV (1914-1922). Benedict had been a diplomat who had served in Church administration all his life. He had not been regarded favourably by Pius X, and had only been made a cardinal three months before the Pope's death. It is said that he found a file in the Vatican denouncing himself on the grounds of Modernism.

He almost immediately turned his efforts to settling the issues of the Great War. To a great extent he was unsuccessful, and both sides in the War distrusted him. He was not allowed to contribute to the Treaty of Versailles which followed the Allied victory.

However, he was able to cancel some of the negativity of Pius X. He allowed Italians to vote and to be involved in the national elections. He discouraged Catholics in Italy from being right-wing political extremists, ready to overthrow the government of the day. He cleared the way for the Italian State and the Vatican to find some common ground. He toned down the Church's own attack on Modernism.

Despite these seeming advances, in 1920 Benedict XV issued an Encyclical letter, *Spiritus Paraclitus*, which took an even more defensive stance than had Leo XIII, some twenty-seven years earlier, regarding the modern methods of biblical interpretation. It was particularly conservative regarding history in the Bible and the historicity of the gospels. One paragraph read:

> If Jerome were living now, he would sharpen his keenest controversial weapons against people who set aside what is the mind and judgement of the Church and take too ready a refuge in such notions as 'implicit quotations' or 'pseudo-historical narratives' or in 'kinds of literature' (*genera quaedam litterarum*) in the Bible such as cannot be reconciled with the entire and perfect truth of God's word, or who suggest such origins of the Bible as must inevitably weaken – if not destroy – its authority.

This went completely against any scholarly approach to the Bible. Benedict XV unexpectedly died of pneumonia in 1922.

### *Pius XI*

The next Pope was Achille Ratti who took the name of Pius XI (1922-1939). He was a renowned scholar, adept in a number of languages. As a diplomat he had come into contact with Communism in Poland and was negatively marked by the experience. After a long Conclave he was elected as a compromise candidate.

His main and immediate task was to solve the 'Roman Question'. This was the ongoing friction between the secular Roman government and the Vatican over the occupation of Rome and the ending of the

Papal States. This impasse between the Vatican and the Italian State was solved in 1929. Discussions had begun in 1926 with Cardinal Pietro Gasparri acting for the Pope, and Benito Mussolini acting for King Victor Emmanuel III. The Lateran Treaty was finally negotiated in 1929 and Vatican City State (including some areas outside the Vatican) was recognised as a sovereign power, separate from the Italian State. Its absolute and sovereign ruler would be the reigning Pope. Restrictions were placed on it: Vatican City must always remain neutral in any military conflict; it could not arbitrate in an international dispute unless all parties requested that arbitration. Reparations were paid to recompense the Vatican for the loss of its Italian holdings, the Papal States, but it could never claim against Italy again. Catholicism was acknowledged as the national religion of Italy (and crucifixes would be placed in all classrooms and government buildings to display that fact!).

Despite all the political manoeuvring, Pius XI found time in 1930 to issue a very stern Encyclical, *Casti Connubii*. It attacked modern views on marriage. It was absolutely against divorce and condemned artificial contraception as 'shameful and intrinsically vicious'. The prime end of marriage was procreation; its secondary end was *unio conjugum* (conjugal love). This Encyclical still stands today as a definitive condemnation of artificial contraception which many in the Church claim can never be revoked. By 1968 the attempt to maintain it would have disastrous consequences.

The world of the time was under the threat of the growing power and menace of Adolf Hitler who assumed the position of Chancellor of Germany in 1933 and led the National Socialist party. The papal nuncio who had been sent to Munich in the 1920s to present the Vatican's position was Cardinal Eugenio Pacelli. Over years he had tried to arrange a treaty between the Vatican and the German government. This treaty would be expected to cover relations between the two states, the rights of the Catholic Church to run its own schools in Germany and the appointment of Catholic chaplains in the German army. Strangely, Pacelli never achieved this until Hitler's time.

Hitler was anxious to gain respectability on the world stage, to be acknowledged by the other European powers. He also wanted to put down opposition to himself in Germany, especially from the Centre Party, which was mainly Catholic. Hitler sent Franz von Papen, the Vice Chancellor, to Rome. Von Papen was a nobleman, but also known as a Catholic. Pius XI did not see Fascism as in principle opposed to the Church; atheistic

Communism certainly was. In the case of Fascism (he had, after all, already come to an agreement with Franco in Spain) he thought he could find a common path with Hitler. Negotiations with Germany followed and a Concordat was signed in September 1933.

But it was not a solution. Pacelli had to protest time and again over violations of the Concordat. Together with some of the German cardinals he drafted a letter of condemnation of National Socialism and Hitler's rule, *Mit brennender Sorge* ('With burning anxiety'). Although written by Pacelli under advice, it carried the signature of Pius XI. Copies were smuggled into Germany and read publicly at Sunday Mass on Palm Sunday, 1937. The Letter condemned the attitude of National Socialism that

> ... exalts race, or the people, or the State, or a particular form of State ... above their standard value and divinizes them to an idolatrous level.

When Pius XI died in 1939 and war clouds were gathering over Europe, his obvious successor was Eugenio Pacelli. The Conclave lasted only one day and Pacelli took the name of Pius XII (1939-1958).

## *Pius XII*

A few months after the Conclave Germany invaded Poland and World War II began. Vatican City declared itself neutral, and this decision was accepted by Hitler. However, Rome was to be occupied by Nazi forces in 1944. While Vatican City State was left unmolested, there were times when it seemed that the Germans would invade it (when, for example, the Vatican gave refuge to Allied airmen on the run). Plans were laid for the Pope to be taken out of Italy but this never happened.

The most contentious issue that has arisen in recent times about Pius XII's reign has been his alleged failure to condemn in a clear way the Nazi treatment of the Jews. In contrast, when the Russians suppressed the Hungarian Revolution in 1956, he published three Encyclicals denouncing the suppression within ten days. Since that time, the Vatican has allowed eleven volumes of papal documents to be released to argue against any collusion of Pius XII in the Holocaust. The matter is still an open debate, but the case against him has not been at all conclusive.

Once World War II had ended, Pius XII took it upon himself to organise aid to the millions of displaced people in Europe. He also argued over the idea of culture in the light of the Nazi claim to an Aryan superior culture. No one culture, one single way of thinking and acting and valuing, is absolute, the Pope stated. He declared his aim to protect local cultures and non-European cultures. As a result, in many cases Catholic missions became dioceses with the mandate to produce their own native clergy and, to some limited extent, to adapt Catholicism to the local ways. Cardinals from Asia, South America and Australia were appointed.

On the other side of the ledger, Pius had to cope with widespread persecution of the Church. After the War in 1945 some millions of Catholics were left under the Soviet regime. Many thousands of Catholic priests were executed or imprisoned for life. The Church was almost eradicated in Albania, Bulgaria and Romania. Likewise in China, at a later date, the Church's base was destroyed after the Communist takeover.

Despite these preoccupations, Pius XII saw the need for the Catholic Church to make a statement on Biblical Studies. The study of the Bible was still a burning problem. In 1941 the Biblical Commission, which had issued no decrees for some two decades, condemned a pseudonymous brochure, whose author was later known to have been an Italian priest, Dolindo Ruotolo. Unbelievably, the brochure was condemned because it was too conservative! It had attacked the scientific study of the Bible and had stated that any study of the biblical text should be restricted to the Latin translation, which was claimed to be more reliable than the original languages. Ruotolo promoted a 'spiritual meaning' derived from the biblical text, one which God directly revealed to the believing reader, rather than any literal meaning. In another age, Ruotolo would have been lauded by a Church that condemned him in 1941; no doubt Pius X would have promoted him.

Ruotolo's spiritual meaning was no better nor worse than the allegorical method proposed by Augustine in the pre-modern worldview nor that used by Pius X. But the Commission was not allowing Ruotolo to go back in time. His condemnation established two principles: that the interpretation of the Bible requires scientific study and that the literal meaning, not some personal spiritual interpretation of the text, is the primary one.

Two years later in 1943 the turning point came for Roman Catholic biblical scholars. In the midst of the horrors of the World War, Pius XII published an Encyclical on biblical studies, *Divino Afflante Spiritu* ('With the Holy Spirit blowing'). He stated (actually the Encyclical was written by a German biblical scholar, Augustin Bea) that the Catholic interpreter of the Bible should be skilled in the use of all relevant scientific methods, making use of the original languages of the Bible (Hebrew, Aramaic and Greek rather than Latin) and concentrating on the literal meaning:

> What is the literal sense of a passage is not always as obvious in the speeches and writings of the ancient authors of the East as it is in the works of our own time. For what they wished to express is not to be determined by the rules of grammar and philology alone, nor solely by the context; the interpreter must, as it were, go back wholly in spirit to those remote centuries of the East, and with the aid of history, archaeology, ethnology and other sciences, accurately determine what modes of writing (*litteraria genera*), so to speak, the authors of that ancient period would be likely to use, and in fact did use.

In short, the Bible was not to be read naively as history. It is interesting that this statement almost pointedly abrogates what Benedict XV's encyclical *Spiritus Paraclitus* had stated in 1920 regarding 'literary forms' (such as myth, poetry, narrative and so on). The only difference was that literary forms, called *litteraria genera* by Pius XII, had been called *genera quaedam litterarum* by Benedict. No doubt, the very subtle change in wording was deliberate. No Pope could directly contradict any earlier Pope.

After *Divino Afflante Spiritu*, Biblical scholars in the Catholic Church felt moderately safe. In 1948 the forward-thinking Cardinal Suhard of Paris put a test question, a Dorothy Dixer, to the Biblical Commission concerning the early chapters of Genesis and the Mosaic authorship of the Pentateuch, matters which seemingly had been definitively decided for Catholics by the Commission at the turn of the century. In a letter of reply, the Commission noted the vast changes that had taken place in the previous forty years. It stated that Moses could not be considered the author of the Pentateuch in the normal sense of 'author', that the Pentateuch was dependent on written sources and oral traditions. Dealing specifically with the first eleven chapters of Genesis the Commission claimed that their literary forms corresponded to no classical categories and could not be described as 'history'. The Genesis narratives related, the letter stated, fundamental truths in a simple and figurative language and gave a popular description of the origin of the human race and the Hebrew people.

The words were liberating to a upcoming generation of biblical interpreters; they completely reversed what had been the Church position some forty years earlier.

The avenues opened by the Encyclical and the 1948 letter of the Biblical Commission, however, were soon to be closed again in 1950 by another Encyclical *Humani Generis* ('Of the human race'). This Encyclical reflected the fear in Rome that Catholic theologians were getting out of hand and was the result of a conservative move in Vatican circles. The Vatican had become aware of the movement dubbed *Nouvelle Théologie* ('New Theology', first used by its opponents). This called for a culturally-aware theology. It also called for a theology that did not depend on official church interpretations and the Scholastic approach to writing theology, but on a return to the sources of the Bible and of early and medieval Church writers.

It is of interest that in that same year Pius canonised his predecessor Pius X and he also declared infallibly that the Virgin Mary had not died but was assumed alive into heaven (a story that seemed undoubtedly metaphorical). There were many in the Church who disagreed with both actions.

*Humani Generis* generally denounced what were considered to be theological deviations. For example, polygenism, the theory that the human race began from more than one ancestor, was censured in this way:

> It is in no way apparent how such an opinion can be reconciled with that which the sources of revealed truth and the documents of the Teaching Authority of the Church propose with regard to Original Sin (the sin of Adam handed down to all humans).

Then, returning to the literary forms of the first chapters of Genesis the encyclical partially retracted what had already been stated in the Biblical Commission's reply to Cardinal Suhard:

> Therefore whatever of the popular narrations have been inserted into the Sacred Scriptures must in no way be considered on a par with myths or other such things, which are more the product of an extravagant imagination than of that striving for truth and simplicity which in the Sacred Books, also of the Old Testament, is so apparent that our ancient sacred writers must be admitted to be clearly superior to the ancient profane writers.

While the reign of Pius XII had allowed Catholic scholars in Theology and Biblical Studies to catch up with their non-Catholic peers, the last years of his pontificate in particular were disastrous and all the advances were retracted. Intellectual development in the Church was paralysed for a long time.

Pius XII was gravely ill for the last four years of his rule. He lost control of church politics in the ever volatile Roman ecclesiastical scene. He claimed to be having mystical experiences and heavenly visions. He spoke with seeming authority on everything. Midwives were instructed on the latest techniques in gynaecology; astronomers heard about sunspots; neurosurgeons were advised on the latest brain surgery techniques. He was, in his own estimation, The Oracle, the infallible teacher and the scholar skilled in all academic fields. His death in 1958 came as a relief to many in the Church.

During the next conclave, the reactionary forces gathered together and devised a strategy which was to put in place one of their own, the jovial John XXIII (1958-1963), Angelo Giuseppe Roncalli, supposedly as a caretaker Pope.

The reactionaries could not have been more mistaken.

## The Conciliar Popes

✠ John XXIII (1958-63)
✠ Paul VI (1963-78)

## John XXIII

John XXIII, formerly a Church diplomat and thereafter Patriarch of Venice, was appalled by what he found in Rome. Power had been delegated by the ailing Pius XII to ecclesiastics who wanted the Church to be the same as that defined at Trent and Vatican I. In an unexpected move (announced to a shocked and unenthusiastic group of Cardinals meeting at a conference in Rome in 1962), John XXIII convoked a new Council to be called Vatican II. He hoped, he said, that it would open up some windows and allow the Spirit to breathe on the church. He used the Italian word *aggiornamento*, bringing the Church up to date and ready to learn from the world and its people. Shock ran through the upper echelons of the Vatican hierarchy.

All bishops throughout the world, heads of male religious orders and some others were required to attend the new Council.

There were many who had thought that there would never be another Council. What could it do? With an infallible Pope who had unrestricted authority, what could a Council achieve? At first it seemed that Vatican II would simply be asked to re-state what had been decided at previous Councils with the addition of recent Papal statements, and that was certainly the aim of the large, conservative faction of Council Fathers attached to Rome. They expected the Council would be over in a matter of weeks. However, there had been strong forces for renewal at work in the Catholic Church for some years and, to the dismay of the Catholic conservatives, they made it clear that they were going to have their say at such a Council.

Vatican II was a chaotic affair. Perhaps all Church Councils had been; it may simply be that we have more written evidence about this one. After the initial announcement of the Council, drafts of statements (*schemata*) were compiled mainly by those in the Papal Curia who lived in Rome. At first they were simply restatements of what Vatican I had already passed, expanded with material taken from the later writings of Popes after Pius IX. Most expected the Council to approve these *schemata* and the Council Fathers could return home.

However, there were pockets of bishops who demanded more say in the *schemata*. There were long debates and discussion-meetings with emotions running high; there was input from experts (*periti*) who were allowed to speak freely. *Schemata* were proposed and then often rejected, sent back for revision or a complete rewriting. There was a political atmosphere that pitted the Roman-based members of the Council against others, whether from Europe or America or the mission fields, although it must be said that many of the Council Fathers had little idea of what was taking place around them.

Understandably, among Catholic biblical scholars there was a grim foreboding when a draft proposal was presented to the assembled Fathers of the Council on the Sources of Revelation (Scripture and Tradition). It was one of the first and appeared in 1962; it was a foundational document, with so much resting on it. It called for restrictions on the research of Catholic scholars; it was something that could have been written in the sixteenth century. The draft was put to the vote: is this draft unsuitable as a basis for further discussion? A two-thirds majority was needed to remove the document completely. Voting was as follows: 1368 yes; 822 no; 19 null. It was not the two-thirds required, but the next day John XXIII intervened and removed it anyway.

The death of John XXIII from cancer, at the end of the first Session of the Council in 1963, raised the question as to whether the Council would continue. Giovanni Battista Montini, the Archbishop of Milan, was the most obvious candidate to be Pope and was duly elected.

## Paul VI

Montini took the name of Paul VI (1963-1978) when elected on the second day of the Conclave. At once, he announced that the Council would continue.

He had been a sickly person in his younger days, so much so that he had completed his priestly studies while still living at home. He became an assistant to Pius XII and, with another priest, ran the Secretariat of State. He was actually involved with the Secretariat of State from 1922 to 1954. He would not accept a cardinal's hat, it was rumoured, because this would mean moving out of the Secretariat. He was reported to the authorities for his liberal religious ideas and Pius XII eventually dispatched him to Milan as archbishop, still without making him a cardinal. Even as archbishop and not a member of the Conclave, some expected him to be elected Pope after Pius XII. That was not to be as John XXIII was elected. In fact, it would be John XXIII who would make him a cardinal in 1959.

With the Council reconvened for another session, the *schemata* came back from revision for reconsideration. Many of these *schemata* had been drastically revised after open debate and input from the *periti*.

Persistently, the question of what would happen regarding the study of the Bible within the Church raised its head. In 1964 the Biblical Commission stirred itself once more and issued an *Instruction on the Historical Truth of the Gospels*. This extraordinary document began with praise for the work of biblical scholars, quoting the admonition of Pius XII in *Divino Afflante Spiritu* that they should be treated with charity. It stated further that the biblical scholar should

> … diligently employ the new exegetical aids, above all those which the historical method, taken in its widest sense, offers to him – a method which carefully investigates sources and defines their nature and value, and makes use of such helps as textual criticism, literary criticism and the study of languages.

The most important section of the document, however, outlined the three stages through which the gospel materials had developed: the actual events of the life of Jesus, the traditions handed on in the early church and thirdly the gospel writers who put those traditions into order and wrote them down. The document, when dealing with the first stage pointed out that the disciples, well equipped to be witnesses of what Jesus said and did, understood his activities as 'deeds performed or designed that men might believe in Christ through them'. It also stated that Jesus' teaching would have followed 'the modes of reasoning and exposition which were in vogue at the time'. At the second stage the apostles would have 'interpreted his words and deeds according to the needs of their listeners' which indicated, of course, that oral transmission had affected the actual form of the traditions.

The document claimed that the evangelists, at the third stage of gospel formation, from the many things that had come down to them from Jesus

> ... selected some things, reduced others to a synthesis, and still others they explicated, keeping in mind the situation of the churches.

This brought joy to the hearts of many biblical scholars. This was full permission to use the 'Higher Criticism' condemned by Leo XIII. In this positive atmosphere the new Vatican II document, a revision of the *schema* rejected earlier, now called *The Dogmatic Constitution on Divine Revelation*, appeared. It assimilated the spirit and even some of the wording of the 1964 Instruction. It left unsolved the long standing controversy between Rome and the Protestants over the sources of revelation, whether revelation derived from two separate sources (the Bible and Tradition) or whether it derived from one source (the Bible as interpreted by Tradition). The compromise is interesting:

> Hence there exists a close connection and communication between sacred tradition and sacred Scripture. For both of them, flowing from the same divine well-spring, in a certain way merge into a unity and tend toward the same end.

At this stage Roman Catholics scholars had more or less caught up with their Protestant confreres in biblical research. The Church was now teaching much the same as Loisy and his fellow Modernists had once taught at the turn of the century.

There was euphoria. This was a new Church led by a new Papacy.

After four sessions (1962-1963; 1963-1964; 1964-1965; 1965-1966), Vatican II ended in 1966. There were approvals for a vast range of documentation, the final forms of the many *schemata*. Bishops, priests, religious men and women and Catholic laypeople were all included in the implications of these final documents.

Bishops were given wider power in their dioceses and they were said to share divine authority with the Pope. Priests were called to re-examine their calling and to adapt themselves to the modern world. Male and female religious orders were instructed to renew themselves and to reconsider their founders' original charism but in a modern setting. Laypeople were encouraged to participate more actively in church affairs. Catholic teaching was expressed less in the juridical and stolid terminology of Vatican I but in simpler terms. In the documents, the biblical text was used, more than ever previously, to explain Church teachings.

One of the Vatican II documents was *The Instruction on Ecumenism*. It explained the unifying aspects of Christianity and maintained that those other Christian churches which were separated from the Catholic Church were still in communion with it, even if in an imperfect way. Despite the statement still being so high-handed, it set the scene for the Catholic Church to become a full participating member of the World Council of Churches. Previously the Catholic Church was only an observer (because it considered itself to be the one and only true Church; how could it be a member of a group of equals?).

So it was that the Catholic Church gave up, at Vatican II, its claim to exclusiveness, at least in theory. It was now officially inclusivist. It was not a simple matter that Catholicism was right and all other Christians were heretical or schismatic. In the main, the term Ecumenism, rarely used in any Papal documents up to this point, indicates due recognition and respect among the Christian religions for each other. While Vatican II only went so far, recognising that there are aspects of truth in the other Christian traditions, it was a vast move forward.

There was also an opening towards the other world religions.

In the first place, amid great controversy, there was an acknowledgement of the closeness between Catholicism and Judaism.

True, the Jewish authorities and those who followed their lead pressed for the death of Christ; still, what happened in His passion cannot be charged against all the Jews, without distinction, then alive, nor against the Jews of today. Although the Church is the new people of God, the Jews should not be presented as rejected or accursed by God, as if this followed from the Holy Scriptures. All should see to it, then, that in catechetical work or in the preaching of the word of God they do not teach anything that does not conform to the truth of the Gospel and the spirit of Christ. Furthermore, in her rejection of every persecution against any man, the Church, mindful of the patrimony she shares with the Jews and moved not by political reasons but by the Gospel's spiritual love, decries hatred, persecutions, displays of anti-Semitism, directed against Jews at any time and by anyone.

Islam, Hinduism, Buddhism also were mentioned, something unthinkable on the Catholic front only a few years earlier. Paul VI made particular overtures to the Greek Orthodox Church. He met with the Greek Patriarch Athenagoras in Istanbul and they mutually lifted their excommunications that had remained standing since 1054. He visited many countries and tried to come to some pragmatic understanding with Communism.

One of the most contentious Vatican II issues was religious liberty. There were violent outbursts among the Council Fathers in St Peter's Basilica as this was debated. In the end there was majority agreement that people had the right to choose their own religion and should be respected for doing so.

Above all, there was a statement on the nature of the Church that overrode the pompous statements of Trent and Vatican I. The document on the Church, *Lumen Gentium* ('Light of the Peoples'), finally decided on this wording to describe it:

> This Church (the Church established by Jesus) constituted and organized in the world as a society, *subsists* in the Catholic Church, which is governed by the successor of Peter and by the Bishops in communion with him.

This was an extraordinary admission – it does not say that the Church of Jesus is the Catholic Church; it does not claim universal authority for the Pope, in fact it only goes part of the way. The document still maintains that the fullness of truth as imparted by Jesus is present in the teachings and practices of the Catholic Church. Where it gives ground is that non-Catholics may have access to that same truth. They may be energised by the spirit of Jesus and their members can achieve salvation. However, the fullness of truth and the full ability to make people holy resides only in the Catholic Church.

The Pope continued to have, the Council declared, supreme authority over the Catholic Church. However, the Council did introduce the idea of collegiality – that the bishops throughout the world share in the authority of the Pope. The bishops would become like members of a board, but the president would remain the Pope. He would be the symbol of unity among them and have the authority and duty to enforce that unity. This notion of collegiality would be later downplayed after the Council concluded.

The Council Fathers either went home or went back to their jobs in the Roman Curia. Life however would never be the same for any of them.

There was hope and enthusiasm among most Catholics as the Council ended. It was the beginning of a New Age, it was commonly said. Education centering on the documents of Vatican II proliferated for priests, for religious, for laypeople; Catholic religious orders held extraordinary meetings to determine the path forward for their particular order. Practices of liturgical observance, of prayer, of personal freedom were reviewed in the light of the new documentation on Liturgy. Paul VI was upheld as the Pope for modern times.

But a dark pall would soon fall on Paul VI's papacy.

From the onset of the Council many Council Fathers had seen the need for a new Catholic statement on birth control. For many of them it was a matter of grave pastoral concern (they were confronted by a people who claimed the necessity of birth control in the modern world but feared the eternal punishment it might bring); for many other bishops the prohibition had meant the serious diminution of numbers in their constituencies, either they be allowed to practice birth control or they would go to another church or no church. Early in the Council, John XXIII, well aware of the seriousness of the matter, had set up a Commission to examine the matter. This Commission was formalised by Paul VI and its membership greatly extended. It would eventually include lay membership. It met six times up to 1965 and reported directly to Paul VI. The question that was posed to the final session of this Commission was: 'Can the Catholic Church teaching on contraception change?'

It was a loaded question. Pius XI had forbidden absolutely any use of artificial birth control in *Casti Connubii*. How would the Commission respond? There were two separate groups in the make-up of the final session of the Commission. One consisted of *periti* from many persuasions including lay members. However, these only had a consultative role (previously, all members had a deliberative vote). The real body of the Commission with a deliberative vote was, for this final session, made up of cardinals and bishops, chaired by the indomitable Cardinal Alfredo Ottaviani, the leader of the conservatives. The vote was as follows: experts – 15 to 4 in favour; the core of Cardinals and Bishops – 16 to 3 in favour with 3 abstentions. They then reported to Paul VI: the teaching of the Church must change; Pius XI's *Casti Connubii* must be overruled.

For some two years Paul VI sat on top of this piece of paper dynamite.

Then Paul VI, whom John XXIII had called 'My Hamlet' because of his constant indecision, made a decision and published an Encyclical Letter *Humanae Vitae*, based not on the majority report he had received but on an unofficial report written by a furious Ottaviani and a conservative American Jesuit, John Ford. It condemned all forms of contraception and used archaic arguments specifically rejected by the Commission. Paul VI had overridden the majority vote of his own Commission.

The principles of Vatican II had not lasted even two years. There was fury, outcry, disputation throughout the Church.

Paul VI died a disillusioned and broken man. He would never publish another Encyclical. *Humanae Vitae* largely ended any enthusiasm for Vatican II as far as many Catholic Church people were concerned. For many this was as far as the Council went. The Church had not really changed; the Papacy had not really changed.

## The Year of Three Popes

☩ Paul VI (1963-78)
☩ John Paul I (1978)
☩ John Paul II (1978-2005)

## John Paul 1

Paul VI was thought to have been considering resignation from the Papacy, but he died in office and was succeeded by Albino Luciani, John Paul I (1978). From the onset John Paul I seemed to be a simple man. A book he had written in Italian, *Illustrissimi* ('Famous People') built on fictional letters to various characters (including Charles Dickens and Pinocchio) became a best-seller. There were rumours that he would revoke *Humanae Vitae*, that he would reform the Roman Curia, that he would investigate the financial scandals at the Vatican Bank.

All this must remain conjectural as he died 33 days after election. There were rumours that he had been murdered, rumours spurred on by the inane attempts of Vatican officials to present his death in a better light (they claimed he had died reading the Imitation of Christ (he died with explosive Vatican documents in front of him); they claimed his priest-secretary had found the body (it had been found by a nun)). The rumours of murder were never substantiated.

## John Paul II

The Cardinals returned again to Rome and they elected a Polish cardinal, Karol Wojtyla, who took the name of John Paul II (1978-2005). He was the first non-Italian Pope since the sixteenth century and a compromise candidate between two Italians, Cardinals Giuseppe Siri (conservative) and Cardinal Giovanni Benelli (liberal), neither of whom could muster the numbers.

He travelled to his native Poland first in 1979 and was received with great enthusiasm. His trip sparked the formation of Solidarity, a trade union movement, the following year headed by a local tradesman, Lech Walesa. This was a workers' union dedicated to promoting freedom and human rights. John Paul supported Solidarity (and almost certainly channeled Vatican money into it) and it became the cutting edge of the struggle for democracy in Poland. For his interventions and support, John Paul is credited with putting an end to Communist rule in Poland between 1989 and 1990. The collapse of Communism in Poland subsequently spread to Eastern Europe in 1990-1991 and to South Eastern Europe in 1990-1992. In 2004 John Paul II was nominated for the Nobel Peace Prize on the basis of his opposition to Communism and his attempt to re-shape a better world.

More broadly, his aim was to re-position the Catholic Church, destabilised after Vatican II and its abrogation by Paul VI. Despite his early experiences as an actor and his involvement in a philosophical study on the human person, he remained at heart a conservative and he wanted to uphold essential Church doctrine at all costs. His fourteen encyclicals pursue the old Church teachings, even though in a more friendly format. As for his teaching on morality, he began with his main concept of the human person:

All human life, from the moment of conception and through all subsequent stages, is sacred.

He took this principle into the scientific field of evolution (where he claimed that there were 'several theories of evolution'):

Consequently, theories of evolution which, in accordance with the philosophies inspiring them, consider the soul as emerging from the forces of living matter, or as a mere epiphenomenon of this matter, are incompatible with the truth about man.

As a result, he condemned evolution, abortion, homosexuality, euthanasia and, for the most part, capital punishment, calling them part of a 'culture of death'.

For many Catholics, however, John Paul II, while claiming to be fulfilling the hopes of Vatican II and implementing them, was seen to have neglected any more progressive agenda that the Council had set in train.

It is true that he made overtures to Anglicans, Lutherans and non-Christian religions, in accordance with the Vatican II decrees. However, he remained adamant on what were seen as key Catholic teachings. In 1995 he published *Ordinatio Sacerdotalis* ('Priestly Ordination') in which he declared that the ordination of women was against core Catholic teaching. No woman could ever become a priest, because the priest must stand in the place of a male Jesus. Many Catholics, male and female, considered then and now that this was a nonsense argument. Women lost confidence in him as this, and indeed much of the sexual agenda of his teaching, seemed to be weighed against them. On the social front, he refused to consider a lifestyle based on Liberation Theology, a marriage between Catholic thinking and Marxism, as a valid Catholic activity even in countries where human rights were openly exploited.

His life, due to his political activities, was put in danger. In 1981 he was shot and critically injured by Mehmet Ali Agca, a Turkish member of the Grey Wolves, a Fascist group. It took place as the Pope was greeting people in Saint Peter's Piazza from his open car. Agca's motives and the foreign backing he received are still a matter of conjecture. The following year a traditionalist but deranged Spanish priest, claiming that the Pope was an agent of the Communist powers, attempted to stab him with a bayonet. Finally, in 1995, when the Pope was to attend World Youth Day in the Philippines, a plot to kill him using a suicide bomber was unmasked by police not long before he arrived.

Due partly to the serious injuries in Saint Peter's Piazza, the energetic and health-minded Pope deteriorated. He contracted Parkinson's Disease in the 1990s. Towards the end of his tenure he was gravely ill and incapacitated. He died in 2005.

### More Recent Times

 ✞ Benedict XVI (2005-2013)
 ✞ Francis (2013 –)

The public funeral Mass for John Paul II was conducted by Cardinal Joseph Ratzinger, Dean of the College of Cardinals. Soon after, he himself was elected in the next Conclave as Benedict XVI (2005-2013).

### Benedict XVI

Benedict XVI was previously an academic and an enigma. He had been a university professor in Theology in Germany. He became better known when he was appointed a *peritus* at Vatican II. Many of the Council Fathers found that he explained difficult issues very clearly and he stressed the need to go back to the sources of Scripture and early Tradition in order to restate Church teaching. His books became obligatory reading for those who were looking for theological newness. For many, as the Council progressed, he was a progressive and liberal and pointed to a new future for the Church.

His liberal openness was not to last. By the late 1960s, after the Council concluded, he was becoming more conservative and his university teaching reflected that. It is said that, in a university setting, he recoiled from the easy-going modern student way of life, the sexual freedom and the attempts to implement Vatican II in a more relaxed form of Catholicism. His last academic appointment was at the University of Regensburg. He then became Vice President of that university in 1976-1977. In 1977 he was made a cardinal and Archbishop of Munich. This was unusual as he had little pastoral experience outside the university sector. His tenure in Munich was not regarded as successful.

In 1981 he was transferred to Rome where he headed for many years the Congregation for the Doctrine of the Faith, once known as the dreaded Congregation of the Holy Office of the Inquisition. By 2002 he was the Dean of the College of Cardinals. It came as little surprise when he was elected Pope after a few ballots.

From the beginning of his pontificate, Benedict XVI demonstrated his very conservative approach to Christianity. He saw relativism, the teaching that human thought and action can only be understood and judged by its human context, as the greatest threat to the Church in this century. He maintained the traditional teachings of the Church, treating the Bible as a mine of facts and instructions. He sternly upheld the decisions on morality, particularly sexual morality, as stated by past Popes. He was against contraception, abortion, homosexuality, divorce, euthanasia. He revived the Latin Mass, which had almost disappeared (he had celebrated the funeral Mass for his predecessor in Latin) and made use of ornate Papal vestments and red shoes. He was out of place in the twenty-first century.

As he grew older and more feeble, there were strident calls for him to act, to do more to revitalise and reform the Church. Young people were deserting the Church in droves, there was a clamor about child sexual abuse by clergy and Church appointees, the Curia in Rome was split into warring enclaves and administration suffered, much was amiss with the management of the finances of the Church in Rome. Immediate and stringent action was needed.

For an old man it was too much. In February 2013 he announced to a shocked world that he intended to resign as Pope. There had only been two resignations previously: Benedict XII and Celestine V. Both have been discussed earlier. Benedict XII resigned under considerable duress imposed by the Council of Constance; Celestine voluntarily resigned, but he had been a most unusual person from the onset; Benedict XVI was simply worn out.

## *Francis I*

Three weeks later, Benedict XVI was replaced, on the second day of voting, by Cardinal Jorge Bergoglio from Buenos Aires who took the name of Francis I. He was to be the first South American, the first Jesuit and the first to take the name of Francis elected as Pope. Being the first Jesuit Pope raised eyebrows: the Jesuits were founded to be the frontrunners for protecting and furthering the work of the Papacy; they were not intended to be Popes themselves. Being South American showed how the Catholic Church's geographical centre of balance had changed. Taking the name of 'Francis' was not clear – did he intend to return to the poverty and simplicity of Francis of Assisi?

*Figure 15*
Pope Francis I

Francis I came to the Papacy with one major question hanging over his head. This referred to the 1970s period in Argentina, when it was governed by a dictatorship. The period has been referred to as the Dirty War, a raging battle between government forces and dissidents, together with some guerilla warriors and some non-violent critics. Thousands had died. At this time, Bergoglio was the provincial superior of the Jesuits in Argentina, no easy task. In 1976 two Jesuit priests were kidnapped and later released after being tortured. A human rights lawyer, in 2005, accused then Cardinal Bergoglio of being complicit in the kidnapping. This has been firmly denied, although there are lingering doubts. Many, including one of the kidnapped priests, have stood up for the new Pope and dismissed any suspicion that he ever collaborated with the regime.

His relationship with the present-day Argentinian government has been ambiguous. He challenged the earlier government of President Nestor Kirchner and was accused of stirring up demonstrations against him. Likewise, he has had difficult relations with his widow and successor, Cristina Fernandez de Kirchner. They have publicly differed on questions such as the distribution of contraceptives, abortion, euthanasia, homosexuality (which he has stated, in the vein of Pius XI and Paul VI, is 'intrinsically immoral') and same-sex marriages, although they had cooperated in protesting about Britain's ongoing possession of the Falkland Islands.

Bergoglio, as Cardinal, kept a tight rein on his clergy and they were told that those in their congregations who defied the Church's teachings on serious moral matters were not worthy of receiving the Eucharist.

> We should commit ourselves to 'eucharistic coherence', that is, we should be conscious that people cannot receive Holy Communion and at the same time act or speak against the commandments, in particular when abortion, euthanasia, and other serious crimes against life and family are facilitated. This responsibility applies particularly to legislators, governors, and health professionals.

Since becoming Pope his statements on Church teaching are a mixture. They have shown a return to a pre-modern form of piety:

> When we do not profess Jesus Christ, we profess the worldliness of the devil... when we profess Christ without the Cross, we are not disciples of the Lord, we are worldly.

However, since his election, he has also made overtures to homosexuals as well as divorced Catholics. He has said that he will not be their judge. Still it needs to be said that his frequent stress on what he calls the great problem of 'spiritual worldliness', when the person puts self in the centre, is very vague as a specific Christian teaching (most if not all religions preach against selfhood!). Claiming this to be the greatest problem facing the Church seems to be rather ludicrous, given the other more prominent problems in the Church and the world.

*In conclusion, at first blush, Pope Francis I appears to be doctrinally and ethically conservative, even if socially aware and progressive. Is this sufficient to save the Papacy? Will 'Peter' take some new form? Will there be a call for a drastic change in 'Peter'?*

*Time will tell.*

# *NOTES*

The amount of material on the Popes and Papacy in the twentieth century is huge. Here are some possibilities:

Coppa, F. (2010), *A History of the Popes in the Twentieth Century: the Struggle for Spiritual Clarity against Political Confusion*, Catholic University of America Press: Washington

Hebblethwaite, P. (1981), *The Papacy in the Modern World*, Burns and Oates: London

For some ideas on the currents of new thinking in the twentieth century, relative to Papal thought, see the exemplary works of Hans Küng.

(1967), *The Church*, Burns and Oates: London

(1983), *Infallible? An Inquiry*, Doubleday: Garden City

(1972), *Why Priests?*, Doubleday: Garden City

and the following:

Miller, R. ed. (2007), *The Future of the Christian Tradition*, Polebridge Press: Santa Rosa

There is also a huge bibliography on Vatican II. These are some examples.

Congar, Y. (2012), *My Journal of the Council*, ATF Press, Adelaide.

This book is a translation of Yves Congar's Diary from Vatican II where he was a well-respected peritus. He ordered it be embargoed until after his death. He speaks frankly about the circuitous ways in which *schemata* were written and amended. He also reveals openly some of the characters, good and bad, at the Council. There are some excellent explanatory essays by modern scholars at the beginning. A warning – it is a long book of some 1000 pages.

Kelly, J. (2009), *The Ecumenical Councils of the Catholic Church: a History*, Liturgical Press: Collegeville

Linden, I. (2009), *Global Catholicism: diversity and change since Vatican II*. Hurst and Co.: London

Malley, J. (2008), *What Happened at Vatican II*, Harvard University Press: Cambridge MA.

Orsy, L. (2009), *Receiving the Council: Theological and Canonical Insights and Debates*, Liturgical Press: Collegeville

# CONCLUSION

This Critical Inquiry into the story of the Papacy has covered a long journey, over two thousand years of the history of the Popes, with so many twists and turns.

At this point we can return, first of all, to the Church Story which built on the Literary Jesus and extended that Story into the related Story of the formation of the Church. Here we are repeating what was stated in the Introduction.

1. Jesus appointed his disciple Simon Peter ('The Rock') as Head of the Twelve Apostles during his lifetime.
2. After the death of Jesus, Peter was confirmed in this office of headship and it was extended to the entire Christian Church by the resurrected Jesus.
3. Peter, after apostolic work in Jerusalem and Antioch, went to Rome and founded the Christian Church there and became its first bishop until he was executed under the emperor Nero. He is buried in Rome.
4. Any successor to Peter as Bishop of Rome is also as a consequence successor to his headship: the successors of Peter, the subsequent bishops of Rome, in an unbroken line, should be accorded the same role of Head of the universal Church as was Peter and their universal authority acknowledged.

The book has shown that there are many problems with any historical validation of this Church Story. Here are some of the problems, which have been mooted in the book:

- Jesus of Nazareth was a Jewish teacher, proclaiming the Reign of God to a Galilean audience and he had nothing to do with the foundation of a separate Church, different to Judaism.
- There is no historical evidence, as against the Synoptic gospels, that Jesus of Nazareth appointed Peter to any office or any succession.
- Peter was never a universal Church leader, never a Roman leader or Bishop, possibly not even a house-church leader.

- There was no monarchic Bishop of Rome until well into the second century.
- It was many centuries before the Pope in Rome even claimed to be the Head of the universal Church.
- There was not an unbroken line of succession of Popes.
- The affirmation of a line of Popes as successors to 'Peter' belongs to the Church Story not to history.

This is the time to return to phenomenology of religion and try to make sense of the two thousand years of the Papacy.

All religions which affirm a High God, distant from the human constituency, have a constant structure:

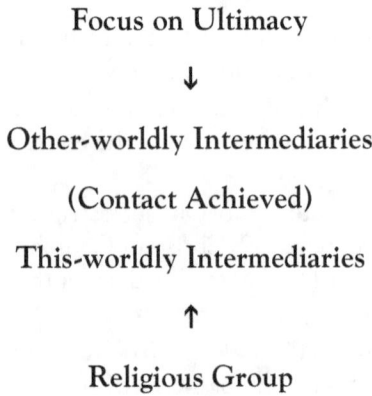

### Focus on Ultimacy

↓

### Other-worldly Intermediaries

### (Contact Achieved)

### This-worldly Intermediaries

↑

### Religious Group

In short, the Religious Group is enabled to make contact with a Focus on Ultimacy by means of its own Intermediaries who actually contact Other-worldly Intermediaries. Some form of succession is required for the line of This-worldly Intermediaries to continue. In the particular case of ancient Israel, this is how the structure worked.

Focus on Ultimacy: The High God Yahweh

↓

Other-worldly Intermediaries: Word of Yahweh,
the Spirit of Yahweh, the Angel of Yahweh

(Contact Achieved)

This-worldly Intermediary: 'Moses'

↑

Jewish Religious Group

The first description of this maintained by Judaism describes Moses entering the Cloud and contacting Yahweh on Mount Sinai. What has been stressed is that such Contact which works for a particular group will pass into oblivion unless some machinery is set up to continue it. In this case it was the nomination of successors to Moses (even if Moses was not an historical figure). Judaism (which this book maintains was only established in the third century BCE) looked back and nominated many in its Literary story: the Judges, the Kings, some great Prophets and, eventually, the Hasmonean Kings. Others looked to the future and identified the new Moses with a figure such as the Messiah, the Just One, the Son of God.

Next we come to the beginning of the Christian period. Instinctively the early Jesus-movement people made subtle changes in this structure. They had been deeply affected by the Jew, Jesus of Nazareth, as they understood him. They adapted the structure to include a new perception of God and, very importantly, a new perception of 'Moses'.

Focus on Ultimacy: 'Abba/ Father

↓

Other-worldly Intermediaries: Word of Yahweh,
the Spirit of Yahweh, the Divine Jesus

(Contact Achieved)

This-worldly Intermediary: The Literary Jesus

↑

Jesus-movement Groups

This worked for the first generation, people who were led by eye-witnesses and disciples. The Literary Jesus (in whatever form, perhaps oral) sufficed. But Jesus was no longer present, no longer visible. Who was the successor to Jesus? Here the Jesus-movement groups put forward a number of possibilities: Peter, James, Thomas, Philip, Judas, Mary Magdalene, 'the Beloved Disciple', Paul. We have seen that, due to historical circumstances, the victor was Peter, combined for some time with Paul. Paul was dislodged and Peter became the sole successor to Jesus. And 'Peter' had his own succession in the line of Bishops of Rome, the Popes.

## Focus on Ultimacy: 'Abba/ Father

↓

## Other-worldly Intermediaries: the Divine Son of God, Jesus (and the Spirit of God)

### (Contact Achieved)

### This-worldly Intermediary: 'Peter' and Successive Popes

↑

## Christian Church

There never was complete agreement among all the Jesus-movement groups that 'Peter' was the Intermediary and never complete agreement that the line of Popes were 'Peter'. However, the mainstream Roman Christianity eventually accepted 'Peter' and most thereafter (but not the East ever) accepted the succeeding Popes as Intermediaries.

However, the shape of the Papacy would change and indeed change in many ways. Here are some of the major changes in shape that the Papacy has taken as seen in our text.

- In the early Church the Popes were pastors, bishops of Rome, who became involved in other churches outside their immediate jurisdiction. Any power came from personal charism. They were similar to successive charismatic leaders of a religious group.
- Constantine and other Roman Emperors made the bishop of Rome the leading Church bureaucrat. This was a change from charism to State office. Such a style was continued with the Byzantine Popes and the Frankish Popes.

- Later, there were aberrations: the medieval families of Rome and Italy who used the Papacy as their private possession and the Avignon Papacy who saw their Papacy as a royal court were examples. In this period Power became the operative word. The Popes were the symbol of political power.
- Exceptions were the reforming Popes who claimed more and more to be not only Intermediaries (whether charismatic or State-employed) but religious/secular rulers with an ever-widening domain. In the end, the Popes claimed to be World Rulers. This was a dangerous claim; it made the role of religious Intermediary murky and increased the dangerous search for Power.
- The Reformation showed clearly that 'Peter' could be found not only in a human successor but in the sacred Book of the Bible. Many Reformers clearly found this new structure more amenable. More about this point will be detailed below.
- The reformed Papacy after the Reformation, was an attempt (not really successful) to re-establish something like a 'Peter', as a charismatic-type leader, separate from the world and its offer of Power.
- However, from the Enlightenment to the beginning of the twentieth century, the Papacy was overwhelmed. It lost, through circumstances imposed on it, any semblance of being a secular potentate and it saw the modern culture as being opposed to it. It was the Outsider in modern society. The Catholic Church became the centre of a counter-culture, fighting against all modernity and trying to shackle its members with fixed thinking and rigid rules. Pio Nono saw himself as the infallible link to the Son of God. From this time the distinctly divine-power character of Pope (together with the Cardinals/Bishops/Priests holding authority) was entrenched.
- The twentieth century forced the Papacy to find peace with modernity (although there were serious lapses). This ended with Vatican II, intending to open the Church to the culture of a new world and to profit by it. It failed. The latter Popes from Benedict XV tried to make themselves World Spokespeople for peace, justice and righteousness. No matter how successful they might have been in this, they were forging a quite different 'Peter' for the Christian Church.

- The Popes since Vatican II have made cosmetic changes and they now continue to see themselves as Spokespeople and Ambassadors. They speak to the world and they are heard in the United Nations; they condemn violations of human rights in the world. They want subtly to reconquer the world for the Church and are willing to make adjustments in order to achieve this.

From charismatic teachers and pastors, the office changed to that of a bureaucrat, to that of subservient adjuncts to Emperors, to claimants to be World Rulers and Renaissance Patrons, to Spokespeople and Ambassadors at large.

As already stated, the great challenge to the Papacy was the Reformation. The religious system underwent a drastic change that persists to the present time with the division of the Roman Church from the Reformed Churches. The Reformers could not see that their religious ambition, to attain contact with the Father, could possibly be furthered by the line of Popes. The Popes hindered them rather than assisting them. They changed the structure.

### Focus on Ultimacy: 'Abba/ Father

↓

### Other-worldly Intermediaries: the Divine Son of God, Jesus (and the Spirit of God)

### (Contact Achieved)

### This-worldly Intermediary: the Literary Jesus (as contained in the Bible, anticipated in the Hebrew Scriptures, fulfilled in the Christian Scriptures)

↑

### Christian Church

At this point the various aspects of the Reformation can be analysed more clearly. There were the desperate attempts on the part of the Papacy to stop the translation of the Bible into the vernaculars, as if the Popes could foresee the possibility of their own displacement. But they were unsuccessful. The Bible became intelligible and substituted for the Pope for so many Reformers.

Within the Catholic Church the Papacy eventually self-reformed in response to the Reformation. It tried to find again something like the simplicity and effectiveness of its beginnings, not always with genuine intent. But, having claimed world supremacy (a foolish claim!), it was challenged by the developing world culture, the Enlightenment and the new world order, and sometimes it responded well, but usually it responded badly. Some Catholic Reformation Popes made valiant efforts but the nineteenth to twentieth centuries were disastrous. That brings us to the present moment.

The Church today is again under challenge and the question is again being asked: Who is 'Peter'?

'Peter', we know from phenomenology of religion, can be whoever or whatever can connect a living Christian community with Ultimacy. 'Peter' can change and must change with the times and the cultures. It is amazing that the Papal institution has lasted, in something vaguely like a continuous form, for two thousand years. But 'Peter' does not have to be a single male, usually a Cardinal, elected by his peers.

The aspects of modern culture that are pertinent to these questions can be identified.

First, there has been general acceptance of a modern philosophy of the human person in society, sometimes explicitly and sometimes implicitly. There is not just one philosophy but many, but there are commonalities among them. The human person cannot be considered unless in some sort of tension with modern culture. We outlined in the Introduction some ideas on human culture. In this Conclusion we present an extension on those ideas to cover a modern approach to the human person.

Humans have a need to put a construction on events in which they are involved and they do so by means of a system of symbols, an everyday culture. They need to construct order, to live an ordered life. Perhaps, some would argue, humans are directed by their genetic make-up to find this order through culture.

Does this vital human culture exist in reality or only in the human mind? It would seem that there is a tendency for humans to situate culture 'out there', in what they would define as reality. It is natural, accordingly, for people to consider their own particular culture to be the 'true' culture, their own way of living is really real; it comes as a shock to realise that there are other humans who regard other cultures as equally valid.

Are cultures comparable? Common, universal characteristics have been confidently identified as existing in all cultural systems. Some have cited the rejection of incest and murder and gregariousness as examples of these universal cultural traits which lead to 'a universal human nature' underlying all human cultures.

There are other scholars who hold that any such universal 'human nature' is illusory. Every culture, they maintain, is unique, formed within the parameters of the life experience of a particular group and variously shaped by non-recurrent historical events. Each element of a culture can only be judged by what it contributes to the totality of that culture. A particular form of government (which is a cultural artefact), such as ancient Greek democracy, or a particular moral stance, such as the condemnation of child marriage, cannot meaningfully be compared to a similar form of democracy or another moral code in another culture, such as one of our Western states; each cultural element only has meaning within the total culture of its own group.

A variant, more moderate relativism has been proposed, and deserves attention. The case could be put that while the behaviour patterns of animals are for the most part genetically determined and the genetic code orders their activity within a narrow range of variation (where does the cat 'learn' its various miaows and their meaning?), human beings are genetically endowed with very general response capacities. These are not cultural universals, they are response capacities which allow humans to learn and to adapt within broad ranges of human activity.

In this sense, we have an innate response capacity or 'instinct' to speak, but our capacity to speak English, for example, is culturally determined. Perhaps this principle can be applied to the whole of culture: capacity is determined and controlled by the biological species; how this capacity will be activated and manifest itself will normally depend upon the culture into which the individual has been socialised. Just as an individual is free to depart from the 'rules' of language and invent neologisms or even speak nonsense, so too the individual can depart from the 'rules' of culture more generally and so behave, think and value in a variant or even a nonsensical way. A human being with capacities only would be an incomplete animal; it is culture that completes the human being by activating these capacities in a quite specific and orderly way.

There is a fear that any form of relativism, including the moderate form described above, will constrain the observer to accept blindly everything proposed in an alien culture. 'Everything' might entail cannibalism, infanticide or female genital mutilation. Moderate relativism does not require its followers to be uncritical of their own culture or even of alien cultures. For a critique of an alien culture to be valid, however, a cultural proposition must be evaluated within its own cultural framework and context, just as it might be critiqued spontaneously by adherents within their own cultural parameters. However, when critiquing an alien culture, its own methods of thinking and evaluating need to be respected. For example, the practice of female genital mutilation cannot be accepted or rejected on any absolutist ethical grounds. It can only be validly critiqued within the cultural context of the, say, north African society in which it is practised as a serious rite of passage.

What does culture, understood in the way proposed, offer to the human being? The human individual has a need for order. To make sense of the cosmos, self and others, the individual within the group requires a direction, a purpose, a basic meaning. All cultural activity takes place in the context of the construction of a cultural 'world' of meanings. These constructed worlds, shaped according to perhaps significantly different configurations of values, power relationships and knowledge, achieve viability because they are supported by a group which, by its general acceptance, gives plausibility to such constructed worlds. The supportive group commits itself to its cultural 'world' and defines its own roles and identities vis-à-vis it. The group members, committed to a culture's constructed world, make sense of human existence through it.

Culture, every culture, offers this advantage to its adherents. In order to find meaning and direction, individuals and groups must accept and then adapt themselves to this cultural heritage of a constructed world. When the group has achieved meaning and direction, it acts to retain its cultural heritage with the same tenacity as an individual displays in maintaining personal, physical life. Hence there is always an element of adherence and continuity in culture, together with a capacity to adapt and change.

It is the universal need for order – the broadest of all general response capacities – together with other human capacities that give rise to the impression of so-called 'cultural universals'. The general response capacities of the human group are activated and directed in different ways by a particular culture. Because of these two factors there will be both diversity and similarity between human cultures.

In short, there is no such thing as the common human person about whom laws, decrees and descriptions can be made. Human persons experience life as problematic. They are confronted by a mass of daily in-formation, by changing values and attitudes. This thinking animal must make a way of life out of this frightening experience. This is done by cul-ture. The human person must choose and must be responsible for those choices; this is human freedom. Where does this human person find a path, build a quality life on the basis of free choice and free response? The person finds these within the self. Each person must find a way of life, a personal culture, and each person is responsible for doing so.

In the Introduction we saw the function of religion as bringing ulti-mate order into a person's life. We have come full circle. The religious structure of Catholic Christianity, with its particular identification of 'Peter', must be seen as one possible way of contacting Ultimacy. And Christian people can do so, the Catholic Church, claims, by means of 'Peter'. This is put forward as an eternal dictum. But 'Peter' has to be considered in changing contexts; 'Peter' can change drastically.

Here, some points need to be made relative to the Papal structure and the changing contexts of the modern Catholic Church.

- The whole idea of a human 'Peter', a single male church-person, who is the Christian Intermediary goes back to simpler times when a local community of moderate size, largely within Rome, sought contact with Ultimacy. A man was chosen to fulfil this need. But 'Peter' does not have to be a man (or a woman). 'Peter' can be a collectivity. The debate over Conciliarism was along these lines. Once the autocratic power of one male claiming to be 'Peter' is challenged, so will the rest of the authority-structure be challenged. The idea of a Cardinal as advisor to the Pope-Em-peror is Roman, making little sense in the modern world. Most importantly, the equality of women in the Church will be an in-escapable result of any dismantling of exclusive male power. Fe-male participation can be achieved in no other way.

- The first requirement of 'Peter' (whatever form is taken) is to adapt in a serious manner to the modern world, to accept the changing fashions of culture in a way that the previous modern Popes were not able to do. The negative decrees of a Pio Nono on modernity must be reversed: the Church must dialogue with modern society, with the ways of the world. The Pope must teach doctrine within the purview of modern culture and the modern view of the human person. This might have been resented in the past; it is essential in the present. Sexual morality (the issues of abortion, divorce, contraception, gender design, homosexuality, same-sex marriage) together with issues of euthanasia, capital punishment and war must be rethought in a new cultural world that has redefined the human person in multiple ways. The past cannot be the criterion. Pius XI spoke on contraception in 1930 with a particular philosophy of the human person: it derived from the medieval idea of a static human nature and was long passé even then and his conclusions were therefore invalid. Paul VI was even more foolish to have protected Pius XI's decision in 1968.

- The theology of the Church, its formal teaching, must be reviewed. Certainly, and necessarily, it must go back to the sources of Scripture and Tradition, but then it must re-state teaching in the new cultural modes of today. The Church teaching on The Trinity, for example, was defined in a particular philosophical and political idiom of the Greek thinking of the Byzantines. Its construction was further deeply affected by political changes on the Byzantine horizon. It has no meaning today for the vast majority of Christians; it should be left to historians. Christians need a new definition of God, of Jesus, of the mediation between Ultimacy and humans, expressed in ways proper to a variety of cultural idioms.

- It appears ever more obvious that 'Peter' must give up the quaint idea of Infallibility. The teaching is irrevocably caught up with a philosophy of static beings. No teaching can continue infallibly and unchanged from era to era or even from one place to another place in the modern world. Guidelines can be given to a global community, but to pretend that any statement can be true for all times and places is to negate the whole notion of human development. It may have been possible for the local Roman church of the first centuries, which shared an ongoing Roman culture, to have defined things in a certain way; those definitions require restatement today.

- Then there is Liturgy, the ritual of the Church. This aspect of the Church must be revitalised or the Church will wither. There is something deep within the human person that requires people to act out ritually what they think and value. Vatican II observed that the Church Liturgy had ossified. It was outmoded, meaningless to so many. Vatican II's own attempts at reform were, sadly, paltry. Meaningless Latin was translated into meaningless English and other vernaculars. One fixed set of rituals were replaced by another fixed set. Ritual requires spontaneity and individuality and therefore difference. 'Peter' must provide the opportunity and setting for such ritual to occur in different ways in different places.

- What of the matter of Church social structure, particularly the priesthood? We have seen that the idea of priesthood evolved over time. It began with the 'elders' of the early Church, moving on, in Roman times and with the adoption of the need for blood sacrifice, to sacrificing priests. When the new idea came into circulation that Christians had been transformed by the sacrifice of Jesus on the cross (not found in the earlier strata of Christian writings) then the sacred meal of the Mass or Eucharist became a sacrifice of Jesus. Eventually it would be described as a cannibalistic sacrifice. However, if there was a Christian sacrifice, then there should be a priest – this was the obvious conclusion by the third century CE. That is what a priest does; a priest sacrifices. Hence, the elders became priests. But, there has always been uncertainties about their role – are they just ministers of the sacrifice enacted in the Mass, or are they also teachers, counsellors, scholars? If the ritual of the Mass is rethought, as it must be, and the notion of sacrifice gives way to the more original idea of meal (given that sacrifice was caught up with specific cultural Roman thinking), so must the priesthood be re-thought.

  There has been further uncertainty about gender. Could a woman become a priest? Perhaps the real question should be: why would a woman want to be a priest in today's ritually inauthentic situation? There was also uncertainty about priestly celibacy. Celibacy was meant to provide a ritually clean human who could approach the real presence of Jesus, his real body and blood, in the Eucharistic Sacrifice. It was also, as we saw, a means of protecting church property from the greed of priests' children. Both reasons seem feeble in today's modern cultures. Priesthood needs to be re-thought, as does the role of bishops and their power-connection with the Pope and the role of cardinals as electors.

- Finally, and perhaps most importantly, there is the great weeping sore of Child Abuse in the Church. 'Peter' cannot ignore it, even if it is not the norm, not the failing of the majority. There are those who say it is systemic. They say it is caused not primarily by the requirement for celibacy of the clergy, but by the search for power by those who feel alienated from Power and find social advancement through the Church's structure. The lust for Power has so often been the scandal of the Church in the past. It has been the root cause of both the many moral scandals of the Popes and the persistence of their personal search for wealth, possessions, absolute political authority and infallibility.

If child abuse is a systemic Church problem, then it is because misshapen human characters (perhaps not a distortion of their own making, it must be added) have sought to have Power and authority over the vulnerable. For reasons that must be examined elsewhere, they have expressed this domination, this need for Power, by sexual abuse. What can be done? If this is systemic, then the answer has to be: close down the whole structure as it stands; not only is it not working, it is inimical to the human person. If it is not systemic, then the evil must be purged at once. The frightening thought is that it may have been the false idea of Absolute Power vested primarily in Popes, but also in Cardinals, Bishops, Priests and certain laypeople that has caused all of this monstrous evil.

*So ends this exhausting Critical Enquiry into the office of the Papacy.*

*There is little doubt that the Popes of the last hundred years or more have been upright and dedicated men. They have displayed weaknesses, but after all they are human. Even 'Peter' was depicted as a flawed person in the Literary Jesus story. But the question goes further than admiring righteous men of good character despite, it must be said, their obvious flaws. Has the time come for a more profound change?*

*Change in the Church must come from within it. The Church is a religious collection of people who are seeking ultimate meaning and direction in their lives. There would be many today who would say that the calcified nature of Church teaching and practice, the persistence of its warped morality and practice of an ineffective liturgy would indicate that there is no or little contact with Ultimacy by means of what the Church is offering. Many Church-goers find ultimate meaning outside the confines of the Church. Immediate contact has always been an alternative. In fact, many people find that the Church is a hindrance, an embarrassment. 'Peter', they say, is not leading the faithful to* religious fulfilment. Catholics are being faced with a 'deus otiosus', a functionless god, and there is a need for immediate change.

As in so many other times, the Church institution itself has to ask: who is 'Peter' today? The answer probably should be quite radical. It is not my place even to make suggestions as to a new structure – that is the role of the Church members. But it seems obvious that something must be done; the answer is not the Papacy as understood today. 'Peter' needs renewal.

## Notes

The ideas on culture refer again to the texts suggested in the Introduction:

Barbour, Ian (1974), *Myths, Models and Paradigms*, Harper and Row: New York.

Geertz, Clifford (1973), *The Interpretation of Cultures*, Basic Books: New York.

Crotty, Robert (1995), 'Towards Classifying Religious Phenomena', *Australian Religion Studies Review*, 8, pp. 34-41.

For a general assessment of the need for change in the Papal structure, with specific reference to Infallibility and the structure of the priesthood, see again:

Collins, P. (1997), *Papal Power. A Proposal for Change in Catholicism's Third Millennium*, HarperCollins Religious: Melbourne.

Küng, H. (1967), *The Church*, Burns and Oates: London

Küng, H. (1972), *Why Priests?* Doubleday: Garden City

Küng, H. (1983), *Infallible? An Inquiry*, Doubleday: Garden City

On Child Abuse see:

Erlandson, Gregory & Bunson, Matthew (2010), *Pope Benedict XVI and the Sexual Abuse Crisis*, OSV Press: Huntingdon, Indiana

Groeschel, F. Benedict (2002), *From Scandal to Hope*, OSV Press: Huntingdon, Indiana

Berry, Jason and Gerald Renner (2004). *Vows of Silence: The Abuse of Power in the Papacy of John Paul II*, Free Press: New York

Jenkins, Philip (2001), *Pedophiles and Priests: Anatomy of a Contemporary Crisis*, Oxford University Press: Oxford and NY.

Tapsell, K. (2014), *Potiphar's Wife. The Vatican's Secret and Child Sexual Abuse*, ATF Press: Adelaide

# Bibliography

*Annuario Pontificio*, (2012), 'I Sommi Pontifici Romani', Libreria Vaticana: Rome

Barbour, Ian (1974), *Myths, Models and Paradigms*, Harper and Row: New York.

Berry, Jason and Gerald Renner, (2004). *Vows of Silence: The Abuse of Power in the Papacy of John Paul II*, Free Press: New York

Browning, R. rev. ed. (1980), *The Byzantine Empire*, Catholic University of America Press: Washington

Bunson, M. (1995), *The Pope Encyclopedia. An A to Z of the Holy See*, Crown Trade Paperbacks: New York

Byrne R. and McNary-Zak, B. eds. (2009), *Resurrecting the Brother of Jesus: the James Ossuary Controversy and the Quest for Religious Relics*, University of South Carolina Press: Chapel Hill

Cameron, Averil (2006). *The Byzantines*. Oxford: Blackwell.

Cameron, E. sec. ed. (2012), *The European Reformation*, Oxford University Press: Oxford

Chadwick, O. (1998), *History of the Popes 1830-1914*, OUP: Oxford

Chiron, Y, (2005), *Pope Pius IX: The Man and the Myth*, Angelus Press: Kansas City

Collins, P. (1997), *Papal Power. A Proposal for Change in Catholicism's Third Millennium*, HarperCollins Religious: Melbourne.

Collins, P. (2000), *Upon this Rock. The Popes and their Changing Role*, MUP: Melbourne

Congar, Y. (2012), *My Journal of the Council*, ATF Press, Adelaide.

Coppa, F. (2010), *A History of the Popes in the Twentieth Century: the Struggle for Spiritual Clarity against Political Confusion*, Catholic University of America Press: Washington

Crossan, J. and Reed, J. (2001), *Excavating Jesus: Beneath the Stones, Behind the Texts*, HarperSanFrancisco: New York

Crossan, J. and Reed, J. (2004), *In Search of Paul*, HarperSanFrancisco: New York

Crotty, R (1996), 'James the Just in the History of Early Christianity', Australian Biblical Review , 44, pp.42-52

Crotty, R. (1995), 'Towards Classifying Religious Phenomena', Australian Religion Studies Review, 8, pp. 34-41.

Crotty, R. (1996), *The Jesus Question. The Historical Search*, HarperCollins Religious: Melbourne.

Crotty, R. (2003). *Beyond the Jesus Question. Confronting the Historical Jesus*, PostPressed: Flaxton, Qld.

Crotty, R. (2012), *Three Revolutions. Three Drastic Changes in Interpreting the Bible*, ATF Press: Hindmarsh.

Davies, Philip (1992), *In Search of 'Ancient Israel'*, Sheffield Academic Press: London and New York

Davies, Philip (1998), *Scribes and Schools. The Canonization of the Hebrew Scriptures*, Westminster John Knox Press: Louisville

Duffy, E. (1997), *Saints and Sinners. A History of the Popes*, Yale University Press: New Haven

Ekelund, R. and Tollison, R. (2011), *Economic Origins of Roman Christianity*, University of Chicago Press: Chicago and London

Erlandson, Gregory & Bunson, Matthew (2010), *Pope Benedict XVI and the Sexual Abuse Crisis*, OSV Press: Huntingdon, Indiana

Estep, W. (1986), *Renaissance & Reformation*, Eerdmans: Grand Rapids

Finkelstein, I. and Silberman, N. (2001), *The Bible Unearthed: Archaeology's New Vision of Ancient Israel and the Origin of its Sacred Texts*, The Free Press: New York and London

Fitzpatrick, M. et al., eds. (2004), *The Enlightenment World*, Routledge: London

Fossier, Robert and Sondheimer, Janet (1997). *The Cambridge Illustrated History of the Middle Ages*, CUP: Cambridge

Freyne, S. (2000), *Galilee and Gospel. Selected Essays*, J.C.B. Mohr: Tübingen

Freyne, S. (2004), *Jesus, a Jewish Galilean. A New Reading of the Jesus Story*, T. and T. Clark International (Continuum): London and New York.

Geertz, Clifford (1973), *The Interpretation of Cultures*, Basic Books: New York

Gregory, Timothy E. (2010). *A History of Byzantium*. Malden: Wiley-Blackwell

Groeschel, F. Benedict (2002), *From Scandal to Hope*, OSV Press: Huntingdon, Indiana

Hale, J. ed. (1981), *The Thames and Hudson Encyclopaedia of the Italian Renaissance*, Thames and Hudson, London

Hasler, A. (1981), *How the Pope Became Infallible: Pius IX and the Politics of Persuasion*. Doubleday: Garden City.

Hebblethwaite, P. (1981), *The Papacy in the Modern World*, Burns and Oates: London

Herbermann, C. et al. eds. (1905-1913), *The Pope Encyclopedia*, RAC: New York.

Jenkins, Philip (2001), *Pedophiles and Priests: Anatomy of a Contemporary Crisis*, Oxford University Press: Oxford and NY.

Kelly, J. (2009), *The Ecumenical Councils of the Catholic Church: a History*, Liturgical Press: Collegeville

Kertzer, D. (1997), *The Kidnapping of Edgardo Mortara*, Picador: London.

Küng, H. (1967), *The Church*, Burns and Oates: London

Küng, H. (1972), *Why Priests?* Doubleday: Garden City

Küng, H. (1983), *Infallible? An Inquiry*, Doubleday: Garden City

Levine, A-J. et al., eds. (2006), *The Historical Jesus in Context*, Princeton University Press: Princeton and Oxford.

Linden, I. (2009), *Global Catholicism: diversity and change since Vatican II*. Hurst and Co.: London

Linforth, K. (2014), *The Beloved Disciple: Jacob the Brother of the Lord*, Vivid Publishing: Fremantle

Lock, Peter (2006). *Routledge Companion to the Crusades*. New York: Routledge

Luscombe, David and Riley-Smith, Jonathan (2004), *New Cambridge Medieval History: C.1024-c.1198*, CUP: Cambridge

Malley, J. (2008), *What Happened at Vatican II*, Harvard University Press: Cambridge MA.

Mango, Cyril A. (2002). *The Oxford History of Byzantium*. Oxford: Oxford University Press

Marcus, A. (2000), *Rewriting the Bible: How Archaeology is Reshaping the Middle East*, Little, Brown and Company: London

Miller, R. ed. (2007), *The Future of the Christian Tradition*, Polebridge Press: Santa Rosa

Orsy, L. (2009), *Receiving the Council: Theological and Canonical Insights and Debates*, Liturgical Press: Collegeville

Stark, R. (2007), *Cities of God. The Real Story of How Christianity became an Urban Movement and Conquered Rome*, Harper One: New York

Stinger, Charles L. (1998), *The Renaissance in Rome*, Indiana University Press: Bloomington

Swanson, R. (1995), *Religion and Devotion in Europe, c. 1215-1515*, CUP: Cambridge

Thompson, Thomas (2000), *The Bible in History. How writers create a past*, Pimlico: London

Thomsett, M. (2011), *Heresy in the Roman Catholic Church: a history*, McFarland: Jefferson, N.C.

Tyerman, Christopher (2006), *God's War: A New History of the Crusades*, Cambridge, MA: Belknap Press.

Wills, G. (2006), *What Paul Meant*, Viking: New York

Yolton, J. et al. (1992), *The Blackwell Companion to the Enlightenment*, Blackwell: Oxford

# Endnotes

1   'Yahweh' is the personal name of the God of Israel. Its origin and meaning is disputed. The older Hebrew text of the Bible has only consonants with some markers for vowels. In the Christian period a full set of vowels were added to the consonants. Because at a later date the Jews did not pronounce this name in their religious services, the text left only the consonants for Yahweh (Y-H-W-H). In those religious services, instead of 'Yahweh' the reader would say '*Adonai* or 'Lord' and so the vowels of '*Adonai* were linked with the consonants of Yahweh to give the impossible word Jehovah.

2   While the God of Israel was occasionally addressed as 'Father', the term was taken on by the early Christians as their particular name for their God (not seen as in any way distinct from YHWH). Possibly the original form was Aramaic '*abba*. The meaning of '*abba* can be 'Daddy', but there is debate as to whether this was the intention of the usage. When '*abba* was translated it became *pater*, which is 'Father' in Greek. More will be said of this later in the main text. The Christian statement on the Trinity refers to the Divinity, in which the Father is one element. The Trinity is a later construction that was motivated by Greek philosophical analysis and a rather protracted and acrimonious political debate. In what follows 'Father' refers to the Christian statement on Yahweh.

3   In mystical religions there can be a more direct approach, an immediate system. For example, in Theravada Buddhism or Gnosticism, where devotees enter into divine space by personal meditation or secret knowledge, Ultimacy can be attained without the need for these Intermediaries. If there is no contact in the mediatorial system (anthropologists talk about a *deus otiosus*, a functionless god) then the mediatorial system can collapse into an immediate one.

4   The differences between Shia Islam and the Sunnis rests on this very point.

5   The Hebrew Scriptures contains, in its present layout, three major sections.

The first section is usually called the *Torah* (its Hebrew title) or the Pentateuch (which means 'five scrolls' or a 'five-part book' in Greek), the first five books of the Bible: Genesis, Exodus, Leviticus, Numbers and Deuteronomy.

The second section of the Hebrew Scriptures, the *Nevi'im* or Prophets, include the following books: Joshua, Judges, 1 and 2 Samuel, 1 and 2 Kings, Isaiah, Jeremiah, Ezekiel and The Twelve Prophets. Not all of these would conform to what we commonly understand as 'prophetic' books.

The third section of the Hebrew Scriptures, the *Kethuvim* or Writings include the following books: Psalms, Proverbs, Job , Song of Solomon, Ruth, Lamentations, Ecclesiastes, Esther, Daniel, Ezra-Nehemiah and 1 and 2 Chronicles.

6   I will not put down the argument for this new approach here, although on the basis of evidence I am most sympathetic towards it. See my book, *Three Revolutions. Three Drastic Changes in Interpreting the Bible*, ATF Press: Hindmarsh, 2012, for more details. The book also justifies the terminology regarding Literary Israel and Literary Jesus which I later use.

7    Scholars who would not contemplate some of the absurdities cited, but still remained committed to Biblical Israel and its methodology would have been William Foxwell Albright, John Bright, Martin Noth, George Mendenhall and their academic heirs.

8    The Samaritans in the north, who had used the name of 'Israel' for their land and were Yahweh-worshippers, were on the other hand removed from participation in this new Israel because of their alleged moral and racial lapses in integrity. They developed separately and were later regarded by the people of the south with great suspicion.

9    We are unsure what the name meant, possibly 'The Hammer'.

10   The Christian Scriptures had been gathered into a definitive and official collection, or canon, by the end of the fourth century CE, twenty-seven books in all. These were composed of the following: the four gospels of Matthew, Mark, Luke and John; the Acts of the Apostles, also attributed to Luke; fourteen letters of Paul, although there was always doubt about his authorship of at least one of them (the Letter to the Hebrews) and today there is widespread agreement that seven of the Letters were composed by Paul, while six are not from his hand; the Catholic letters, so-called because they were presumed to be not addressed to particular communities but to the universal (in Latin, *catholica*) church – the letter of James, two letters of Peter, three letters of John, one letter of Jude; finally, the book of Revelation. As with 'Old Testament', 'New Testament' is no longer politically correct since it presumes that Judaism has been superseded by Christianity. We will see later that the canon of the Christian Scriptures was finally decided when Roman Christianity had survived all other forms.

11   See my books already mentioned, Three Revolutions. *Three Drastic Changes in Interpreting the Bible*, particularly chapter 15 and, in more detail, *The Jesus Question*.

12   This is a description of the final edited version of the Gospel of John that circulated in Christian Churches affiliated with Rome. The origins of the Gospel of John are a much more complex question.

13   Flavius Josephus (37-100 CE) was a Jew, regarded by fellow Jews as a renegade because, in the struggle against Rome, he went over to the Roman side. He became the protégé of the Roman general, Vespasian. When Vespasian became Emperor in 69 CE he adopted Josephus and Josephus took on the family name of Vespasian's dynasty, Flavius. Josephus then wrote in Greek two principal books: *The Jewish War* in about 75 CE and *The Antiquities of the Jews* in about 94.

14   For some substantiation see my books cited in the bibliography.

15   This depicted an Exodus-in-reverse from Israel into the Land to Egypt (which rouses suspicions that the description is a theological treatise, based on the Moses analogy, not an historical narrative).

16   The latter were compromised by the fact that they were collaborating with the colonial enemy, collecting taxes on their behalf and hoping to extract more so they could provide for their own households. Taxes were slowly grinding the Jewish populace into penury.

17   The Sadducees were one of the sects of Judaism in the first century CE. They were conservative and politically powerful in contrast to the Pharisees. The Pharisees accepted new interpretations of the Torah; the Sadducees did not.

18   This identification of the Christian Gnostic with Jesus explains how Judas Didymos Thomas, the supposed author of the Gospel of Thomas, could be known as the The

Twin (*Didymos* is Greek and *Thomas* Aramaic for 'twin'). He was the spiritual replica of Jesus.

19   The figure is confirmed by the text of the *Res Gestae*, an account of his great achievements by the first Emperor, Augustus.

20   Mithraism was a Persian religion that had made its appearance in Rome sometime in the first century BCE.

21   The *Liber Pontificalis* was written in Latin but at an uncertain date. A first edition covered the names and achievements of the Popes from Peter up to the ninth century. New editions took the list to the fifteenth century.

22   *The Apostolic Constitutions* were probably collected and written between 375-380 CE. The author is unknown. In the main they provide a manual of practice for Christian clergy.

23   Literally, the 'Fifth-Sixth' Council since it intended to complete the work of the Fifth, one held earlier.

24   Although at this distance the impasse between Pope and Emperor over using the image of the Lamb to depict Jesus may seem trivial, there were meanings in the Lamb symbol that caused distrust in the East.

25   In fact, Constantine had given only the Lateran Palace to the predecessor of Sylvester I, Miltiades (311-314), and had begun the construction of the original Saint Peter's Basilica, which became Papal territory. But there was no more territory granted.

26   Benedict IX appears on this list three separate times, because after his initial election he was once deposed and restored, then once sold the Papacy and then retrieved it.

27 This however was not the shortest Papal reign. The list of short-lived Popes is as follows:

Urban VII (1590): reigned for 13 calendar days

Boniface VI (April 896): reigned for 16 days

Celestine IV (1241): reigned for 17 days

Theodore II (897): reigned for 20 days

Sisinnius (708): reigned for 21 days

Marcellus II (1555): reigned for 23 days

Damasus II (1048): reigned for 24 days

Pius III (1503): reigned for 27 days

Leo XI (1605): reigned for 28 days

Benedict V (964): reigned for 33 days

John Paul I (1978): reigned for 34 days.

28   Paul VI was the last Pope to be crowned with a tiara. He later sold it and gave the proceeds to charity. Since then there has been no tiara in the ceremony that acclaims the election of a Pope.

29   Celestine V's was the first papal resignation. There have been other claims but they are not sustainable. Pope Ponzian was arrested by the Roman Emperor in 235 CE and sent to the salt mines from which there was no return. Rather than resigning he most probably was presumed dead. Pope Marcellinus is also sometimes said to have resigned. More likely he was deposed for apostasy in 304 CE. Likewise, Pope Liberius was said to have resigned in 352 CE, but in fact he was exiled and an Antipope, Felix

II, installed in his place. He returned to Rome and lived side by side in the city with the Antipope. Then it is claimed that John XVIII resigned in 1009 but it is more likely that he was deposed and illegally replaced by the powerful Crescenti family in Rome. His last days were spent in a Roman monastery. The only other resignations were Gregory XII in 1417 (of which later) and Benedict XVI in 2013.

30    He must not be confused with the twentieth-century Pope of the same name.

31    His resignation would be the second after Celestine V and the next resignation would be Benedict XVI in 2013.

32    Pope Francis has reversed this trend towards noble quarters and has moved into the nearby guest-house.

33    While Peter is sometimes accredited with a Papal reign of some 37 years, he was neither Pope nor long-lived in Rome. The list of long-reigning Popes is as follows:

Pius IX (1846–1878): 31 years
John Paul II (1978–2005): 26 years
Leo XIII (1878–1903): 25 years
Pius VI (1775–1799): 24 years
Adrian I (772–795): 23 years
Pius VII (1800–1823): 23 years
Alexander III (1159–1181): 21 years
St. Sylvester I (314–335): 21 years
St. Leo I (440–461): 21 years
Urban VIII (1623–1644): 20 years

34    Later, on the fortieth anniversary of the writing of this Encyclical, Pius XI would write another letter, *Quadragesimo Anno*, bringing this social teaching up to date and this was repeated by John Paul II on the hundredth anniversary of *Rerum Novarum*, with his own encyclical *Centesimo Anno*.

35    'Lower Criticism' is the science of restoring the original text of the Bible and removing deliberate or unintended errors, if that is possible. Leo XIII had no problems with this. 'Higher Criticism' (also known as the historical-critical method) was used to ascertain the text's original meaning in its original historical context. It also sought to reconstruct the historical situation of the author and recipients of the text.

# INDEX